I0038757

The Story of
ii' taa'poh'to'p

UNIVERSITY OF CALGARY
LCR Publishing

The Story of ii' taa'poh'to'p

University of Calgary's Journey Towards an Indigenous Strategy

Grandparents of ii' taa'poh'to'p

This is a symbol for the smudge. The square at the bottom represents a smudge altar in the tipi. The smoke rises from the altar towards the sun. For this book, this symbol is parallel to a copyright symbol [©] for western publications.

© 2025 Grandparents of ii' taa'poh'to'p

LCR Publishing
An imprint of University of Calgary Press
2500 University Drive NW
Calgary, Alberta
Canada T2N 1N4
press.ucalgary.ca

All rights reserved.

This book is available in an Open Access digital format published under a CC-BY-NCND 4.0 Creative Commons license. The publisher should be contacted for any commercial use which falls outside the terms of that license.

LIBRARY AND ARCHIVES CANADA CATALOGUING IN PUBLICATION

Title: The story of ii' taa'poh'to'p : University of Calgary's journey towards an Indigenous
  strategy / Grandparents of ii' taa'poh'to'p.
Description: Includes bibliographical references.
Identifiers: Canadiana (print) 20250182076 | Canadiana (ebook) 20250184923 | ISBN 9781773856278
  (hardcover) | ISBN 9781773856285 (softcover) | ISBN 9781773856292 (PDF) | ISBN 9781773856308
  (EPUB) | ISBN 9781773856315 (open access PDF)
Subjects: LCSH: University of Calgary. ii' taa'poh'to'p. | LCSH: University of Calgary—Planning. |
  LCSH: University of Calgary—Administration. | LCSH: Indigenous peoples—Education (Higher)—
  Alberta—Calgary. | LCSH: Universities and colleges—Alberta—Calgary—Sociological aspects. | CSH:
  Indigenous college students—Alberta—Calgary.
Classification: LCC LE3.C32 S76 2025 | DDC 378.7123/38—dc23

The University of Calgary Press acknowledges the support of the Government of Alberta through the Alberta Media Fund for our publications. We acknowledge the financial support of the Government of Canada. We acknowledge the financial support of the Canada Council for the Arts for our publishing program.

The manufacturer's authorized representative in the EU for product safety is Mare Nostrum Group B.V., Mauritskade 21D, 1091 GC Amsterdam, The Netherlands. Email: gpsr@mare-nostrum.co.uk

Copy editing by Dallas Harrison
Cover design, page design, and typesetting by Melina Cusano

Front cover image: Buffalo image gifted to *ii' taa'poh'to'p* by Amelia Crowshoe, BCC'09, JD'20.
  ii' taa'poh'to'p cultural model, designed and transferred to UCalgary by Reg Crowshoe Hon, LLD'01.
Back cover image: Backside view of *ii' taa'poh'to'p* tipi. June 29, 2018. University of Calgary.
  Photo credit: Riley Brandt, UCalgary.

Special Honouring

We would like to take this opportunity to remember and honour the lives and contributions of the late Kainai ceremonial Elder and spiritual adviser Andrew Black Water [Aa tso towa] and Dr. David Lertzman. Their spirit and strength are at the heart of *ii' taa'poh'to'p*. Their words of wisdom and encouragement continue to guide us in a good way.

Final Pipe Ceremony. Kainai Elders the late Andy Black Water (left) and Calvin Williams (right). June 21, 2017. University of Calgary. Photo credit: Riley Brandt, UCalgary.

The late Dr. David Lertzman and Elder Reg Crowshoe at the Inner-City Community Dialogue. October 17, 2016. Fort Calgary (now called The Confluence). Photo credit: Riley Brandt, UCalgary.

Contents

ii' taa'poh'to'p count designed by Reg Crowshoe.

A traditional winter count [isstoksistimaan] is a visual representation of events where the winter represents a year, and each symbol is a "count," representing an important event or events for that year. All the symbols put together create a visual oral narrative of events over a series of years. For this book, the symbols represent each of the chapters, capturing our journey towards the development of *ii' taa'poh'to'p*. This *ii' taa'poh'to'p* count is visually parallel to a table of contents.

Central Symbol
The central symbol on the *ii' taa'poh'to'p* count represents the Indigenous strategy and the Office of Indigenous Engagement, symbolized by a chickadee nest and leaders within the institution who are responsible for the Indigenous Strategy.

Chapter 1: Understanding the Landscape
This is a symbol of a scout; the half circle above represents the top of a hill, and the straight line down indicates that it is safe to travel.

Chapter 2: Setting Out
Together, these symbols represent the beginning of a journey—a dog travois and travellers, packed and ready to set out on our journey.

Chapter 3: Coming into the Circle
These symbols represent all of creation being invited into a circle, signifying an ethical space.

Chapter 4: Our Four-Stage Journey
This symbol represents four distinct lodges or spaces to be visited. Each tipi represents one of the four stages of our journey.

Chapter 5: What We Heard
These symbols represent dialogue between a storyteller/orator and a listener, and the exchange of knowledge between them.

Chapter 6: Creating the Strategy
These symbols represent Indigenous and non-Indigenous people working together on the development of the Indigenous strategy; the symbol of the smudge in between the two groups represents the creation of a safe and ethical space. The symbol of the bundle on a tripod represents *ii' taa'poh'to'p*.

Chapter 7: Empowering the Spirit of ii' taa'poh'to'p
The buffalo at the centre of the circle is the symbol for education (our new buffalo); the circle represents an ethical space. The two symbols below represent the youth/learners coming into a safe learning environment (the university) where everyone is welcome.

Chapter 8: Reflections
This symbol represents water and our reflection in the water.

Transformation through Relatives

From 2010 to 2018, I oversaw the development and implementation of an academic master's-level program in social work based on Indigenous knowledges. This program was an extension of my professional and academic career focused on tackling the suppression of Indigenous knowledges and practices in social work education and creating spaces for the resurgence of Indigenous ways in the academy and the profession of social work. My work in the academy was based on the conviction that to truly create necessary change in the relationship between Indigenous peoples and newcomers—who have been arriving for generations—we have to generate learning opportunities for newcomers. This work focused on helping newcomers to see the remarkable contributions and abilities of Indigenous peoples and ensure that they have the space and freedom to build upon their knowledge systems. Through the development of good, ethical relationships between two distinct cultures and the implementation of cultural parallel practices between Indigenous peoples and all others in Canada, our society as a whole will bring to life the many dreams that we have for ourselves, our children, and the generations to come. As an Indigenous scholar, educator, and social worker, I knew that a key way to initiate change was through the education system, specifically within postsecondary institutions, which are deeply influential in laying the foundation for our future generations.

In the fall of 2017, I came across a call for applications for the role of vice-provost of Indigenous engagement at the University of Calgary. Through this call, I was able to review the university's Indigenous Strategy entitled *ii' taa'poh' to'p*, released in November 2017. I thought that this was one of the most intriguing, mindful, and thorough calls by a postsecondary institution for Indigenous engagement and reconciliation. I was fortunate enough to be hired and started in the role in June 2018. To this day, I see *ii' taa'poh'to'p* as a truly visionary and necessary document. It is this vision—encompassing key concepts such as parallel paths, shared ethical space, transformation, and renewal as well as ways of knowing, doing, connecting, and being—that has guided units and faculties throughout the university. In this way, the whole university—from the Board of Governors and General Faculties Council to various faculties and administrative teams—is engaged in contributing to the institution's journey toward truth and reconciliation. Clearly, the campus community is wholeheartedly taking on the recommendations outlined in *ii' taa'poh'top*.

The strategy has led our institutional commitment to transformation and renewal, with the significant involvement of Traditional Knowledge Keepers and ceremonial Elders. The implementation of a Circle of Advisers made up of Elders and senior administrative members is a key recommendation of the strategy and an ongoing structural change at the University of Calgary. This circle provides opportunities for senior members to engage Elders on high-level developments within the university. It also acts as a way for the university to confirm its commitment to Indigenous engagement and to the Indigenous community.

Most of the Traditional Knowledge Keepers and ceremonial Elders who helped to develop *ii' taa'poh'to'p* continue to work with the university, and many more have joined us on the journey and been involved in a variety of meaningful ways. In any particular year, close to one hundred Traditional Knowledge Keepers are actively involved in advising, contributing ideas, teaching, and supporting students, staff, and faculty members. These Elders have supported many key developments. One of the many examples is the development of the Landscape Plan, which provides guidance on the university's physical landscape over the coming twenty-five years. Other developments include the creation of Indigenous spaces in many faculties; increased financial and individual supports for students; new courses, content, and programs addressing Indigenous peoples and perspectives; more events and activities focused on Indigenous ways of knowing, doing, connecting, and being; assessment and approval of new and redeveloped academic programs; and contributions to renewed and emerging institutional policies. Many of these activities and events have contributed to increased learning opportunities for students, staff, and faculty members.

Since the launch of *ii' taa'poh'to'p*, transformative initiatives have continually increased and expanded in meaningful and impactful ways. These innovative ways of doing and connecting include nurturing academic partnerships, honouring Indigenous peoples and experiences through large community events, and facilitating respectful research partnerships with Indigenous communities. These few highlights reflect a cultural shift from a culture of exclusion to one of reciprocity in Indigenous engagement. With these transformative endeavours, Indigenous people are more engaged with the university, as evident by the ever-increasing numbers of Traditional Knowledge Keepers/ceremonial Elders and Indigenous students, staff, and faculty members.

I would be the first person to say that we are only just beginning and that, as outlined in *ii' taa'poh'to'p*, these are the first steps on a journey of transformation, which continues to require an ongoing and renewed commitment to reconciliation. As someone who has committed more than forty years of my personal and professional lives to Indigenous education and inclusion, I can say—without a doubt—that I am honoured to be a member of an institution demonstrating its commitment to walking a parallel path of transformation and renewal for all people of the University of Calgary and beyond.

Dr. Michael Hart,
Kaskité-mahihkan , ᑲᐣᑭᑌ ᒪᑯᐦᑲᐣ , Black Wolf

Preface

In March 2016, the University of Calgary, under the leadership of the Office of the Provost, embarked on a journey toward the development of an Indigenous Strategy. This journey began with the creation of an Indigenous Task Force composed of a Steering Committee, an Elder Advisory Group, and a Working Group representing the diverse faculties and services of the university. Each group had documented Terms of Reference outlining key roles and responsibilities. However, realizing that this approach did not adequately reflect Indigenous perspectives, members of the Task Force worked with Traditional Knowledge Keepers to create a parallel process based on an Indigenous framework. This parallel path was called "Journey toward the Indigenous Strategy." The Indigenous Strategy *ii' taa'poh'to'p* is grounded in cultural teachings shared by the Traditional Knowledge Keepers and/or Elders engaged in the development of the strategy who helped to guide and inform our collective journey.

Land Acknowledgement

The University of Calgary is located in the heart of southern Alberta, the traditional territories of the Peoples of Treaty 7, which include the Blackfoot Confederacy (comprising the Siksika, Piikani, and Kainai First Nations), the Tsuut'ina First Nation, and the Stoney Nakoda (including the Chiniki, Bearspaw, and Goodstoney First Nations). The City of Calgary is also home to the Métis Nation of Alberta (Districts 5 and 6). The university is situated on land northwest of where the Bow River meets the Elbow River, a site traditionally known as Moh'kinstsis to the Blackfoot, Wîchîspa to the Stoney Nakoda, and Guts'ists'i to the Tsuut'ina. On this land and in this place, we strive to learn together, walk together, and grow together "in a good way."

Opening Smudge

In honour of our parallel journey and the story of *ii' taa'poh'to'p*, we open this story space with a smudge as validation of our story circle, our journey together, and the process of collective truth telling. According to Traditional Knowledge Keeper Dr. Reg Crowshoe, a

> Smudge is an introduction to a system; it constitutes our copyright. Smudge honours the land. Land is physical representation of our natural laws. Acknowledge that our society has governance and laws—circle includes all dialects. The circle is all inclusive and provides a relational framework of how to work together. When I go back to our Indigenous knowledge, the story of the smudge came from interaction of creation. . . . Smudge also creates a place of safety, a place and way of doing things in a good way.

About This Book

The Story of ii' taa'poh'to'p is a narrative account of the development of an Indigenous Strategy at a large university in Canada, the University of Calgary. This book captures and shares many stories of our collective journey to develop the strategy as well as the lessons learned along the way. Foundationally, it is a story of the development of intercultural respect and understanding and of making good relatives. The strategy was developed at an important time in the history of Canada and the university, a time of truth and reconciliation and deep reflection. We wanted to write this book to ensure that the stories were captured and shared, for we believe that we took a unique approach to our journey, one that will have a lasting impact on our institution and great potential to help others with their journeys toward reconciliation.

Dru Marshall

The interaction of collective creation becomes knowledge. The purpose of writing this book was that we thought we needed to capture the knowledge and share our journey of creating the University of Calgary Indigenous Strategy. We have a responsibility to pass on our knowledge by sharing our story. If anyone wants to use the four-stage-journey method, there is due diligence—the need to work with the local Indigenous community and protocols thereof. When we brought the Elders together for our strategy, we had Elders from the Treaty 7 region and the urban centre. We called upon older "traditional" systems that provide a communal way of working together through the basic principles of circle, language, smudge, and story. When we come together in circle, the smudge and pipe are tools used to understand each other. Organizations must work with the local Elders or Traditional Knowledge Keepers in their community. We may have a method and a practice that can be interpreted; however, it needs to be adopted within a local cultural context.

Reg Crowshoe

This amazing story captures the emergence of a framework, dynamic processes, creative and innovative tensions, and ultimately thoughtful and respectful actions that honour parallel paths—Indigenous and non-Indigenous traditions. All have been waiting patiently, sometimes impatiently, to be awakened to begin the work of conciliation, realize reconciliation, and foster the promises embedded in the treaties and agreements among the Indigenous peoples (First Nations, Métis, and Inuit) of these lands, educational institutions, the Crown, and Canada. *ii' taa'poh'to'p* is a gift to the University of Calgary and much more. The awakened spirit is paving a new path at the university and invites us to see the spaces within it with heightened senses and through new eyes—as intertribal and inclusive, clear and real, and ready for constructive, systemic, and healing changes. This journey has resulted in institutional practical wisdom, invaluable organizational knowledge, and a new and daring vision for those children not yet born, seven generations into the future.

Jacqueline Ottmann

Narrative Style

This book follows a collective storytelling framework. The essence of truth lies in collective experiences and stories told from multiple perspectives. It is through these collective experiences that understanding and relationships crystallize. In honour of Indigenous and non-Indigenous ways of sharing, this book reflects oral storytelling practices. The layout of the book includes important transitional stories as we move from one chapter to the next. We also introduce each chapter with four short stories that reflect the content of the chapter.

For Piikani Elder Dr. Reg Crowshoe, four stories are linked to a ceremonial framework and can be envisioned as "alignment stories, offered in ceremonies when a new part of the ceremony begins":

> The inclusion of four alignment stories at the beginning of each chapter is a core part of our circular journey. As lessons are shared and new knowledge is learned and built, the process is shared as a storied journey, moving through different levels of storied experience enriched by learned lessons and teachings. Each time understanding and practice are learned, it is time to go to another level, accompanied by another four stories that you take with you as teachings. In that way, the circle and its stories drive a lifelong cyclical or spiral learning process enriched and deepened by storied experiences of the people. In this light, it is also important to think about the nature of circles and the four stories as more than just a way of organizing knowledge. When these four stories are shared within the circle, the process reflects an oral narrative of creation. That is, it creates new knowledge in addition to sharing existing knowledge. And in that process there is a power, a jurisdiction, and a spirit. These are what give Indigenous knowledge and ways of knowing an inalienable, equal standing with Western knowledge.

Crowshoe explains that, from a parallel lens, the four stories are analogous to a preface for each chapter and help to set the context for it. The offering of the four stories signals the next stages of the ceremony or, in this case, the progressive stages of the collective journey toward the development of *ii' taa'poh'to'p*. This storied format was also informed by Shawna Cunningham's (2022) dissertation, which included the four alignment stories—based on teachings from Crowshoe—further enhanced by the addition of related creative prose, serving as transitional stories placed between each of the chapters.

This book offers important oral teachings that invite deep reflection. These teachings were fundamental to our transformational journey and learning process. We encourage you to read each teaching and reflect on it before moving on to the next chapter. Each of you will take different meanings from the lessons articulated in the oratories, but each interpretation will help you to understand the importance of and the processes underlying the development of an authentic Indigenous Strategy.

You will find a circular and thus repetitive approach to the book. Many Elders share certain stories repeatedly to emphasize a teaching or concept. The concepts fundamental to this story are realizing the importance of Indigenous knowledge systems, creating parallel paths, inclusion of Indigenous voices, relating storied experiences, and making time to develop respectful relational processes.

Preface Stories

CONFORMITY

When I was really young, my first education was of the language, the circle, and the Little Birds [a learning society]. That's how I viewed the world. So, in the nest, when they make the smudge, they say we transform all of you into Little Birds. And when you all become Little Birds with your friends, we all accept each other, and we all work together, and we become relatives. So, in that context, I was transformed through the concept of sanctified kindness and building relatives. That was my buy-in to a system. I want to be a part of a system that nurtures my skills for learning and that will help me to transfer my knowledge. I want to be a part of that because the system is inviting you through the concept of building relatives and sanctified kindness, so it's easy. And that's how I transformed into the nest and all the other circles after that.

So, when I translate that, I would say there was a time when I was delivered to the residential school. And when I got to the residential school, I really didn't have a clue about any kind of education laws. I didn't understand what a classroom was. I didn't understand sitting in rows. I didn't understand what a blackboard was. I didn't understand what a bell was to get the class going. I never understood any of that. So, when I came to the school, my first scare was seeing the kids running around having fun in the schoolyard. And I enjoyed that with the kids, but then somebody was ringing the bell at the door of the school, and the kids all started running. And I thought, "Whoa! Something is happening." And when you flee like that and run, then you'd better be scared for your life. So I ran back to my grandmother.

So then, when I was in the classroom, I was asked for my name. So I gave them my Indian name, Áwákaasiina [Deer Chief], and I was punished for it. I was beaten up for it. I was smacked by the teacher, and I thought she hit me because I wasn't talking loud enough. So I yelled. Then I got smacked again. And this time I was lying on the floor in front of all my community kids. It was a shock. It was—how would I say—confusing. It was an embarrassment. It was all those feelings. So, at that point, I realized my cousin was standing with me, and he told me in Blackfoot "kinchihka'sim." And then, when I heard that, I knew what I did wrong, because he told me I couldn't speak Blackfoot. So I locked up all that Blackfoot knowledge (my relatives and teachers and circles) in my head and did not talk about it. The reason I did that was that I was going through a transformation of another form. It was a transformation through conformity. I realized that, if I didn't conform, then this [punishment] is what's going to happen, so I had to conform. That was the written education policy from the Indian (Act/Agent) to the residential school that we had to follow. And that was transformation by conformity.

So I experienced two types of transformation [as a child]: transformation through building relatives and transformation through conforming. So, when I talk to organizations about a transformational framework, I always go back to my easiest/kindest option, and that is building relatives so that we can work together to survive rather than building something you have to conform to because then you're going to get into scaring people. That's what I always look at. It's building relatives to transform versus transformation by conformity. You're putting options out there. You don't want to be looking at [enforced] system change because people are going to ask "Why do I have to?" There's going to be resistance. So why not use the option of building relatives as a buy-in to a system of survival together in achieving a goal? So, when I understood that we were going to work with the whole institution, the University of Calgary, I thought, "Whoa, we need to work with the framework of building relatives."

Reg Crowshoe

CHOICE

I've been a member of the Indigenous Strategy Steering Committee for the past few months. Although I joined later in the process, I've witnessed an incredible amount of passion, innovation, and dedication in the efforts of both the Working Group and the Steering Committee.

As just one of two university graduates (my sister being the other one) in a large Métis family, I personally recognize the need for strategies that enable Indigenous achievement in higher education as students, teachers, and researchers. The Truth and Reconciliation Commission Report and associated Calls to Action give us a choice. We, as Canadians, now have to choose to do something to improve the relationship with Indigenous peoples, or we choose not to improve the relationship; ignorance is no longer an excuse for inaction.

To me, the culturally appropriate and innovative approach to the development of the Indigenous Strategy that Dru, Shawna, Jackie, and Jacqueline with Reg Crowshoe and the other Elders have employed is unique to the University of Calgary and speaks volumes to the commitment the institution has to working toward an improved relationship. The dual paths of the cultural model and the standard strategic document help to connect ways of knowing and behaving. Between those two paths is the space where dialogue and relationships are built and strengthened. The strategy development has lived up to its guiding principle of "Together in a Good Way: Journey of Transformation and Renewal," and I firmly believe this principle should carry on through implementation and integration with the current Eyes High and future university strategies. I believe the Indigenous Strategy will mark an important milestone in the U of C story.

Kris Frederickson—member,
University of Calgary Board of Governors, 2017[1]

---

1   Content based on an email addressed to Dr. Dru Marshall, June 23, 2017; shared with special permission.

Transitional Story

BLACKFOOT STORY OF THE SMUDGE

When I go back to our Indigenous knowledge, the story of the smudge came from the interaction of creation. When I look at interaction within the spirit world, the mystical world, and the real world, I would look at jurisdiction and how those three worlds interact. In the Blackfoot stories, a hero from one of our community camps was Scarface. He was living in a camp that had hard times—a lot of famine—and even he personally had a hard time. He was being bullied in the community as a child; he had a scar on his face. He went to a Creator's Lodge, which is in the spirit world. It's a long story, but eventually he vowed to go to Creator to have his scar removed. He went all the way through the real world, the mystical world, and then to the spirit world. When he got there, he had Creator clear off his scar. Creator healed him in a sweat. Creator took the feather and wiped off the scar with the feather while they were in the sweat. We called that action of wiping the scar off Scarface's face Somiikan. His name then changed from Pii'ak'ski to Somii'on. The story went on that Creator told Somii'on, "When you came all the way to the spirit world, to the Creator's world, you came because of your hardships and the hardships you're having with your camp—your famine, your sickness, your deaths—and the hardships you're having with your whole people are represented in that scar. So I've cleared off the scar with my feather." Then Creator told him "The sweetgrass represents the concept of a sanctified kindness of all our relatives." Anything that is created is our relative. So the sweetgrass is my relative. The buffalo, the water, the air, and the stars—those are all our relatives.

Creator said that the sweetgrass represents the concept of sanctified kindness. His instructions were to "take a hot coal from the fire and put it down, and then take the sweetgrass—which is sanctified kindness for all creation—and put it on the hot coal; then the smoke will come up." The sun represents Creator's world. It's hot in the morning, and when you smudge it is like Creator taking the scar off you. The smoke comes up from the smudge, and your hand becomes a representation of the feather that Creator had to take the scar off Scarface. So you take the sweetgrass, put it on the hot coal; when the smoke comes up, you put your hand over the smoke, and you cleanse yourself. You transform yourself into a safe space to have a gathering, so you can learn or make decisions. We all go through the act of cleansing ourselves.

After that sweat was done, Scarface brought the sweetgrass back home. When he came back from the spirit world or the sun's world—which is also Creator's world—back to his community, he brought the sweetgrass. So that's the basic understanding of our call to order. We make a smudge as a call to order, but the smudge builds the understanding that everything in creation is our relative, and we must enact that sanctified kindness so that we can take away whatever or what isn't working for us to make right decisions.

Oral Teaching, Piikani Elder Reg Crowshoe

Understanding the Landscape

Dru Marshall, Shawna Cunningham, Jackie Sieppert,
Jacqueline Ottmann

Four Stories

TWO SYSTEMS

My grandmother would say "Creator gave the [Western] written system their administration, and they gave the oral [Indigenous] system their administration. They're both equal, but we have to acknowledge them like the wampum belt with two canoes—not crossing each other. And if we can do that, then we can work together."

Reg Crowshoe

MUTUAL UNDERSTANDING AND RESPECT

This strategy is not about integration or assimilation. It is not because we find comfort in being the same but because we find inspiration in being different. It is about two cultures walking parallel paths—beside each other—and creating ethical space between us that allows for authentic dialogue to unfold to develop mutual understanding and respect. It is not about the next five-year period but about how we mutually coexist—together—well into the future.

Dru Marshall

A STORY OF HOPE

This Indigenous Strategy was a dream come true for many Indigenous people who were and are connected to the University of Calgary—students, staff, faculty, Elders, leaders, and community members. We heard stories of hope, anticipation, and longing to be recognized, acknowledged, and appreciated in ways that uplifted and centred Indigenous ways of knowing, being, connecting, and doing. The energy generated by the process of creating the strategy was tangible and highly motivational. We had the sense that we were on the cusp of something significant for the University of Calgary—that a shift was about to happen. The whole process was purpose driven.

Jacqueline Ottmann

MOMENT OF ENLIGHTENMENT

There was a moment of enlightenment early on. We were sitting in circle with the Elders at Red Crow Community College, and we were asking for guidance on the development of the strategy. We shared what we were planning to do and how we were hoping to approach the strategy. The late Kainai Elder Andy Black Water provided some words of wisdom and guidance that really resonated with those of us who were there to listen. He said something like this: "Whatever you do, don't create something that people are afraid of. Don't create something where people look at us with pity. We don't want to be pitied. We have pride in our cultural ways, and we want to be engaged. We want to be part of something." These words resonated throughout our journey.

Shawna Cunningham and Jackie Sieppert

Our Intent

Our intent in writing this book is to share our story about the development of the University of Calgary Indigenous Strategy, capturing our ongoing journey toward reconciliation and our path toward becoming and maintaining good relatives through a lens of reciprocity. We tell the story from both an organizational and an individual point of view. The University of Calgary embarked on an intentional and inclusive two-year journey to develop our Indigenous Strategy, now called *ii' taa'poh'to'p*. We undertook our journey in relationship with, and guidance from, Indigenous people, leaders, and community partners to ensure that we proceeded in "a good way." Early on, the university decided to develop the strategy through cultural parallels. Parallel conceptual and cultural models were designed and developed as a conscious commitment to the process of reconciliation in all forms but with an intentional focus on educational reconciliation. We learned several lessons along the way that we thought were timely and important to share given the call for reconciliation in Canada. Although we are an educational institution, we believe that these lessons are transferable to other organizations embarking on their own journeys toward truth and reconciliation.

This book reflects our lived experiences through evaluative and reflective lenses. We hope that you find valuable teachings within the book that will both inspire and inform your own journeys. In the spirit of truth telling, we also wanted to share the struggles and tensions encountered in our organization, and within ourselves, as we completed this journey.

We have written this book in a way that allows you to navigate the content how you choose. You can move back and forth to different places in the book. Certain concepts also emerge repeatedly. As in teachings by Elders, we tell and retell stories to reinforce the concepts and to add depth and breadth to them. These concepts include the importance of systems of Indigenous knowledge, parallel paths, storied experiences, Indigenous voices, and time to develop respectful relational processes.

We hope that you enjoy the journey!

Our Starting Point

Historically, and throughout Canada, increased representation and mean-ingful inclusion of Indigenous students in higher education were most often the result of emergent Indigenous initiatives such as Native Studies programs, student access programs, culturally relevant student services/centres, and community-based recruitment. These initiatives often un-folded in relation to one another in Canadian postsecondary institutions (Pidgeon et al. 2013). Together, these initiatives actively demonstrated to the community an institution's commitment to create a place of welcome, inclusion, and cultural relevance for Indigenous students, community members, and knowledge systems. For Indigenous students, cultural relevance is noted when institutions offer a wide variety of high-quality Indigenous-focused academic programs and courses, culturally informed holistic services, designated gathering spaces for Indigenous students and community members, a visible active and reciprocal presence in Indigenous communities, hosted cultural events of value to the commun-ity, and an active meaningful presence of Indigenous faculty and staff. These markers speak to wise practices, demonstrating an institution's commitment to Indigenous people's education and meaningful inclusion. Indigenous representation in public postsecondary education is what most institutions tended to strive for both before and after the release of the *Final Report of the Truth and Reconciliation Commission of Canada* (TRC 2015). However, without an overarching institutional Indigenous Strategy, the good initiatives listed above often happened in silos or were fleeting in nature, responding to an immediate need rather than a sustain-able long-term vision. The following passage from the former director of the University of Calgary Indigenous student centre and co-author of this book is a reflection on the changes noted at the university since the early 2000s and after the launch of the Indigenous Strategy:

> In November of 2000, I was hired as the director of the Native Centre (now Writing Symbols Lodge), the University of Calgary's Indigenous student support services centre. Upon arrival, I was handed a mandate that included not only the provision of culturally relevant student services for Indigenous students but also recommendations for the centre

to be responsible for the administration of an existing transitional program offered on site at a First Nations college, a directive to create and offer a similar campus-based transitional program and manage Indigenous community relations and engagement on behalf of the institution. What I experienced when I arrived in the role was not outside the norm in public postsecondary institutions. Alongside existing Native Studies programs, the centres were known as institutional hubs for indigenization on campus, commonly operating with limited financial and human resources and broad mandates. In 2000, there was no formal process in place for Indigenous students to self-identify. Indigenous representation was not a focused priority in higher education at the time. Additionally, there were maybe two or three full-time self-identified Indigenous faculty members and a handful of Indigenous sessional instructors. Indigenous people were generally under-represented.

Since the launch of the Indigenous Strategy in 2017, representation at the University of Calgary has steadily increased, with admissions, access, and bridging programs for Indigenous students and strategic inclusive hiring practices for Indigenous faculty and staff. There have been three cluster hiring programs for Indigenous scholars and special incentive programs to attract Indigenous postdoctoral scholars. Collectively, these latter two initiatives have resulted in Indigenous-led and -focused research.

In terms of academic programs, the university has some well-developed innovative programs that started to unfold in the early 2000s. In 2002, the Faculty of Social Work launched its community-based learning circles program, offering a tailored Bachelor of Social Work (BSW) degree in partnership with selected rural communities and First Nations colleges. For the BSW program offered in First Nations communities, community instructors and Elders were engaged in curriculum development and delivery, enriching the curriculum with Indigenous worldviews and languages. In 2004, the university launched a minor in International Indigenous Studies, which grew into a full degree program offered through the Faculty of Arts. The Faculty of Education (now the Werklund School of Education), upon request from the community (e.g., Siksika Nation, Tsuut'ina Nation, Stoney Nakoda Nation), also began offering professional development and degree programs on site and in partnership with select First Nations colleges at both the bachelor level and the master level. These kinds of continuing education, community-based programs, and academic partnerships have continued to grow since the launch of the Indigenous Strategy, with a more mindful approach relative to community reciprocity and what constitutes an equitable partnership in academic programming and inclusion of Indigenous pedagogies in teaching and learning. We must go far beyond a transactional partnership model to a more relational model, so there is much more work to be done in this realm.

Preceding the university-wide Indigenous Strategy document were faculty-based Indigenous Strategies, such as the Werklund School of Education's Indigenous Strategy, *Moving Forward in a Good Way*. This strategy was unanimously passed by the faculty council in March 2015 (three months before the national TRC report was released) after two years of collaboration, community consultation, writing, and verification. The president and provost paid close attention to this process and others within the university for insight into successful strategic frameworks involving Indigenous relatives.

Prior to the launch of the Indigenous Strategy at the University of Calgary, most of the well-intentioned efforts to be more inclusive of Indigenous people, practices, and pedagogies unfolded in isolation from each other and were not sustainable. There was no overarching institutional commitment or strategy to guide and coordinate our work "in a good way" that would last long into the future.

Grounding Ourselves

We embarked on our developmental journey by familiarizing ourselves with the landscape to better shape and inform our process. This required an understanding of key national and international documents and our current institutional climate (strategic environment) to better articulate the rationale, significance, and process of creation for an Indigenous Strategy and to determine institutional readiness.

GUIDING DOCUMENTS

Our journey toward the creation of an Indigenous Strategy for the university was "guided by documents that recognize common themes and recommendations, based on the principles of community and institutional capacity building within the current socio-cultural landscape" (University of Calgary 2017b, 34). There were three key documents:

1. the final report of the Royal Commission on Aboriginal Peoples (RCAP) (Government of Canada 1996);

2. the United Nations Declaration on the Rights of Indigenous Peoples (UNDRIP) (United Nations 2007); and

3. the *Final Report of the Truth and Reconciliation Commission of Canada,* Volume 1 (TRC 2015).

The following excerpt from the *ii' taa'poh'to'p* document provides an overview of these guiding documents:

> The Final Report of the Truth and Reconciliation Commission of Canada released in 2015 . . . builds upon the work of [the] Report of the Royal Commission on Aboriginal Peoples and the United Nations Declaration on the Rights of Indigenous peoples in impactful ways. Over a six-year period, the Truth and Reconciliation Commission of Canada conducted hearings across the country, serving as witnesses to the stories of residential school survivors and their families. The Truth and Reconciliation Commission's final report was over five hundred pages, which included 94 Calls to Action. The calls to action challenged individuals, organizations, and institutions to take an active role in the process of reconciliation. These calls to action include several clear statements pertaining to education and the inclusion of Indigenous peoples and perspectives in teaching, learning, and research. The Commission called notably for the following measures: Indigenous course content and cultural awareness training to become mandatory; funding must be provided to integrate Indigenous epistemologies, methodologies, and pedagogies into classrooms; a dedicated

senior-level leader should be responsible for the facilitation of Indigenous content in education; educators and students must be made aware of the legacy of residential schools and the assimilationist policies of the past; community Elders and Indigenous spiritual beliefs should be integrated into educational programming; and a funded national research program should advance the understanding of reconciliation.

The United Nations Declaration on the Rights of Indigenous Peoples (UNDRIP, 2007) also serves as an important foundation for the University of Calgary Indigenous Strategy. The UNDRIP asserts that Indigenous groups have the right to control and establish their own educational systems and have linguistic and cultural autonomy. UNDRIP also asserts that Indigenous people have the "right to all levels and forms of education of the State without discrimination" to be provided "when possible" in their own language.

The Final Report of the Royal Commission on Aboriginal Peoples, released in 1996 after five years of inquiry and deliberation, insisted on the necessity to define a new contract with Indigenous people that would respect the principle of "nation to nation, people to people relationships." The Report also emphasized the critical importance of traditional knowledges, Elders, and Indigenous spirituality, and how these are often ignored in Canada's education system.

In response to the TRC, Universities Canada, which represents 97 universities across Canada and educates more than a million students each year, agreed to mandate 13 principles for Indigenous education. The 2015 Universities Canada report began by recognizing that Indigenous students continue to be underrepresented in Canadian higher education institutions. This issue was identified as an urgent issue for Canada. Universities Canada argued that closing the educational gap will strengthen Indigenous communities, contributing to self-determination, the informed citizenship of Canadians, and Canada's long-term economic success and social inclusion. Universities Canada declared that higher education offers great potential for reconciliation and a renewed relationship between Indigenous and non-Indigenous people in Canada. It also suggested that the "cohabitation" of different scientific approaches and methodologies on campuses, including in priority Indigenous knowledges, has the power to open a dialogue between people of diverse cultural groups, enhancing our shared knowledge. (University of Calgary 2017b, 35–36)

These grounding documents served as road maps, guiding and affirming the importance and value of education for Indigenous people, the importance of relationships between Indigenous and non-Indigenous people based on mutual respect and benefit, and the meaningful inclusion of Indigenous ways of knowing, being, and doing. Our journey was informed by the recommendations in these documents and affected by the Indigenous stories of the experience of colonization, including human and Indigenous rights violations, current socio-cultural inequities, racism, and genocide. Each of the documents alludes to or directly identifies parallel development as the way forward for building or rebuilding our spaces and places—our organizations, institutions, and societies—and for beginning or restoring relationships.

STRATEGIC ENVIRONMENT

Some institutions in Canada started to envision and launch Indigenous Strategies prior to the release of the *Final Report of the Truth and Reconciliation Commission of Canada* in 2015. In 2010, Simon Fraser University, for example, was one of the first institutions to launch an Indigenous Strategy. The release of the Truth and Reconciliation Commission's report shone a much-needed national spotlight on the dark history of colonization and the resulting socio-cultural gaps between Indigenous and non-Indigenous people in Canada in all sectors of society. The report incited an overarching call for *Reconciliation through Education* (see NCTR 2024) combined with numerous specific calls to action targeted at the transformation of postsecondary education systems and programs. As the honourable Dr. Murray Sinclair, the former chair of the Truth and Reconciliation Commission of Canada noted, "education is what got us into this mess and education is key to getting us out of it" (NCTR 2024). The development of the University of Calgary Indigenous Strategy started in late 2015. This late start, as some would say, was an advantage since our work was motivated and informed in part by the *Final Report of the Truth and Reconciliation Commission of Canada*, and we were able to learn from other postsecondary institutions from across the country that had already launched Indigenous Strategies.

In addition to examining the external environment, and grounding ourselves in the key documents described above, we assessed the internal environment by asking ourselves who are we? Where do we come from? Where are we going? What are our responsibilities? Having a clear understanding of the overall strategic direction of our institution was an important starting point. The University of Calgary is one of Canada's leading research-intensive universities—a young, bold, and dynamic institution that embraces opportunity. A reflection of the city in which it resides, the university is consistently highly ranked in national and international assessments. The success that the university was experiencing in 2015 was driven largely by a commitment to the inspirational and aspirational *Eyes High Strategy* (see University of Calgary 2017a), first developed in 2011, re-energized in 2017, and concluded in 2022.

The *Eyes High Strategy* set the bar for forward momentum at the university, and two accompanying operational documents, the Academic and Research Plans, served as road maps to achieve the vision. In 2012, ten priorities were identified between the two plans, and these priorities guided all human, capital, and financial resource allocations on campus. Together, the *Eyes High Strategy* and Academic and Research Plans were used to drive annual plans, set agendas at both the Academic Senate and the Board of Governors meetings, describe institutional impacts in government reports, and respond to government and community requests. In this way, strategic planning and action at the University of Calgary were highly integrated.

The Academic Plan had seven priorities, one of which was *connection with community*. Within that priority, connections with Indigenous communities were identified as a key objective. The Academic Plan also highlighted that,

> as a result of the focus on the identified academic priorities, graduates of the University of Calgary will have experienced high quality, engaging academic programs and will

be thoughtful, communicative citizens and leaders of their respective communities, with abilities to think critically and creatively to solve issues of the day. They will understand the value of collaboration and partnerships and will be used to working with others who are considered traditionally outside of their fields of expertise. They will also appreciate different cultures and see value in diversity—of opinion, thought, gender, race, and culture. They will appreciate the limited resources available on Earth, and work and live to create a sustainable future. (University of Calgary 2017a)

We understood that we had to reimagine and rebuild our relationships with Indigenous communities.

The Academic Plan drove the production of several subplans, including international, sustainability, teaching and learning, and mental health strategies. In addition, as part of our overall strategy, in late 2015 the university embarked on a journey to establish an Indigenous Strategy.

WHY AN INDIGENOUS STRATEGY?

It was within this broader external and internal strategic context that the Indigenous Strategy was undertaken at the University of Calgary, particularly to connect, in meaningful and transformational ways, the university to Indigenous peoples[1] and communities. Indigenous peoples have been consistently under-represented, and Indigenous knowledge systems have been continuously dismissed and misinterpreted in university settings. Indigenous peoples, generally and historically, have not been well supported and set up for success within colonial education systems (TRC 2015), including universities. In our strategy, we noted that

the clear and compelling imperative for the development and realization of the University of Calgary's Indigenous Strategy is based on an authentic foundation of compassion encouraged through cross-cultural learning opportunities that promote awareness, education, and understanding. Building

---

1   We use "Indigenous peoples" as an inclusive term to refer to the First Nations, Métis, and Inuit Peoples in Canada.

knowledge and understanding of Indigenous perspectives, worldviews, histories, cultures, and belief systems is essential to enabling and realizing steps towards true reconciliation between Indigenous and non-Indigenous peoples. Educational institutions have a profound responsibility in initiating, securing and sustaining reconciliation. (University of Calgary 2017b, 2)

The Indigenous Strategy also served as the institutional response to the TRC Calls to Action (2015) and to other major reports written years earlier, as noted above (see Government of Canada 1996; United Nations 2007).

INSTITUTIONAL READINESS

At the University of Calgary, we were used to developing and implementing strategies and plans and, by most measures, successful in doing so. However, it was clear that the process to develop an Indigenous Strategy would be different. Key lessons learned during this strategic process related to ways of doing: Indigenous peoples are generally relational and emphasize transformation, whereas universities tend to be siloed and transactional. Universities rely on written tradition, whereas Indigenous peoples follow oral tradition that spans generations to transfer and safeguard knowledge. Universities rely on set Eurocentric rules and procedures to conduct meetings and engage in decision making, whereas Indigenous peoples rely on cultural protocols and oral practices (e.g., smudges, pipe ceremonies, songs) to open, guide, and close decision-making processes in "a good way." Institutional ways of doing rely on processes of payment not congruent with Indigenous protocols for honouring and gifting Traditional Knowledge Keepers (e.g., tobacco, blankets, honoraria). There was much for all to learn, and it took time to do so. Where most strategies had been developed in six to eight months, the Indigenous Strategy took nearly two years. We took that time because we wanted to get it right. We engaged in a parallel process that honoured both Indigenous and non-Indigenous ways of doing, being, connecting, and knowing. We did not want to create a strategy about assimilation or integration. Rather, we wanted to engage in a more respectful and inclusive process by building an understanding of cultural parallels and then walking parallel paths on our journey toward developing the Indigenous Strategy.

Importantly, we had to re-establish—and in some cases establish—relationships with Indigenous peoples. We were fortunate to have a group of respected and wise Traditional Knowledge Keepers who were patient and willing to take the time to work with us to ensure success of the strategy. While committee members who worked on the strategy went through significant personal and professional education, it did not take long for us to realize that our institution—board members, faculty, staff, and students—also needed to be educated. We found through our processes that there was a general lack of knowledge about Indigenous peoples in Canada and, in some cases, blatant discrimination and racism against Indigenous students, scholars, and staff. These were among our darkest days. Despite a prevalent climate of intercultural illiteracy across the institution, we persevered and encouraged everyone to learn Canadian history, and the history of these lands prior to settlement, from Indigenous perspectives— history that we all should know through the experiences and traditional teachings of Indigenous peoples but were not taught in our colonial education systems.

Because of the focus on the Truth and Reconciliation Commission, we were more ready institutionally in 2015 than we would have been in 2012, but we still had a long way to go. There was an increased awareness of Indigenous issues, but we lacked an overall institutional understanding.

INSTITUTIONAL STRUCTURE FOR STRATEGY DEVELOPMENT

Strategy development at the University of Calgary typically involved a task force composed of a Steering or Management Committee (eight to ten people) and a Working Group (thirty to forty individuals). The Steering Committee, usually co-chaired by a member of the executive team, along with a senior professor who is an expert in the strategic thrust, was responsible for the overall direction, establishing terms of reference for committees and ensuring that documents were ready for the approval processes within the university. The Working Group, usually co-chaired by a member of the senior leadership team and a staff member with significant expertise in the strategic focus, was responsible for obtaining and processing information, writing and editing key documents, and carrying out the direction provided by the Steering Committee. All strategies involved significant internal and external community consultation. In the case of the Indigenous Strategy, Traditional Knowledge Keepers were added to the development structure and became important and integral members of both the Steering Committee and the Working Group.

Once a strategy is developed and deemed ready for the process of approval, there are two branches of governance approval at the University of Calgary. In the first instance, the strategy is approved by the academy. This requires that the document be taken through several subcommittees, typically twice, once for discussion, and once for recommendation for approval, on the way to the Academic Senate of the university. This iterative process is educational, resulting in improved strategies as feedback from the academic community is incorporated as the documents move through the process. Once approved by the Academic Senate, the strategy is also approved by the Board of Governors. In a fashion similar to the academy, the document is moved through several subcommittees of the board—again twice—prior to formal approval by the full board. Following approval of both the Academic Senate and the Board of Governors, there is a formal launch of the strategy, to which both internal and external community members are invited to attend. In the case of the Indigenous Strategy, Traditional Knowledge Keepers and Indigenous scholars and leaders were present at Academic Senate and Board of Governors meetings to provide support, advice, and guidance related to systems of Indigenous knowledge and ceremonial ways. In addition to university approval processes, Indigenous ceremonial validation was invoked throughout our journey as part of our parallel approach.

Sharing Our Journey

As we share our journey of the development of the University of Calgary Indigenous Strategy, now called *ii' taa'poh'to'p*, we do so in a parallel way by sharing cultural teachings, our personal narratives or storied experiences, excerpts from the strategy document, and lessons learned along the way. The creation of our Indigenous Strategy was unique since we included Traditional Knowledge Keepers in the developmental structure. They grounded and shaped our developmental journey and infused and animated the strategy document through Indigenous ways of knowing, doing, being, and connecting.

The next chapters follow a journey format. The chapter called "Setting Out" focuses on how we embarked on our journey. "Coming into Circle" shares key epistemological teachings from Traditional Knowledge Keepers, embedded in the strategy and shared through conceptual and cultural frameworks. "Our Four-Stage Journey" describes our journey framework and the parallel paths that we walked to create the strategy. "What We Heard" recounts our community dialogues that helped to inform and shape the strategy. "Creating the Strategy" addresses how we approached, reflected on, and compiled thematic content of the strategy based on what we heard. "Empowering the Spirit of *ii' taa' poh' to'p*" shares our parallel process of institutional approval, ceremonial validation, cultural celebration, and implementation. The chapter titled "Reflections" captures transformational moments, milestones, challenges, and lessons learned.

Transitional Story

OLD CAMP, NEW CAMP

When we were talking about the strategy at the university, I was wondering how do a group of people transform, and how does that transformation come about? What's the story? So, as I thought about oral narratives of knowledge, I came upon the one that we use. That was the Lone Chief story about moving to new camp. So how did we move to new camp and include the environment and everybody that we were related to? There were three camps involved: old camp, present camp, and new camp. How did they all move and change, and how did those three concepts come about? New camp is what we always tried to get to, because we're always at present camp, and we all came from old camp. When I was listening to the story, there was an old-timer and an old lady one time who were in present camp. When the group decided to move to a new camp, they were getting to the age where they couldn't haul their stuff, and they needed help. Everybody got ready and started moving. The scouts had already gone out to find someplace safe where they could temporarily camp until they got to the new camp. So the old man and old lady were caught being last. And in them days, they travelled with dog travois. One of their dogs, a female, just had pups, and they couldn't take the pups with them, and they couldn't use the female on the journey, so they just left them there. They took what they could—their tipi and all that—and left whatever else was there. They then followed the whole camp to the present camp.

When they all got there, the old-timer was thinking about his dogs. "I left my dogs and some of my stuff at old camp," and he was talking about relatives and how he let them down, how he couldn't look after them, and so on. He felt bad about it. So the next morning he told the old lady, "Well, we're going to be here a few days, so I'm going to go back and see if I can find the dogs and some more of our stuff, and they can come back." So he went back to old camp. When he got back to old camp, all that was left, and all he could see, were the tipi rings of the lodges in the camp. He knew where his lodge was, but there was just the tipi ring left.[1]

So it was in the evening, and he called his dogs—the female and the pups—but none of them was around. So he made a fire and made himself something to eat. He said, "Well, I'm going to sleep where I used to sleep. Even though there's no tipi, it's a warm night. I'm just going to sleep outside." So he had something to eat. Then he left some food out for the dogs in case they came, and he went to sleep. In his sleep, he dreamt that he was in his tipi. The tipi was up, and he was home. And this young man came in, and he said, "Lone Chief is inviting you to a feast and a dance." And the old man said, "Okay, tell Lone Chief I'll be right there." And then he went out, and he thought to himself "I'm too tired. Maybe I'll skip this one." And he lay down again. Then another young man came in and said, "Lone Chief's inviting you." So four times he was asked. In our way, if you're asked four times, then you have to go. So, after the fourth request, he said, "Oh, okay, I guess I have to go, because there's four of them." And that's where that cycle of four was represented.

He followed the last young man, and came out of his tipi, and walked across camp. All the other tipis were up. He followed them into Lone Chief's camp. When he went in, it was a big camp. Lone Chief sat up front with his wife, and all the other young men were on each side. He went in, and Lone Chief asked him to sit beside him. He sat up at the front beside Lone Chief. Lone Chief said, "All these young people came together to help the old people. The ones who are having a hard time. You should have asked us. When you guys were going to move, you should have told us that you didn't have help. We would have given you help." And then he said, "But now, tonight, we're going to make it formal. We're going to have our relatives come in." And the relatives were all the animals and plants. "They are going to come into this lodge, and we're going to put together a framework of an organization, a society, so this society can go with your camp, and we use it [the society] to help all the old-timers." So they formed what they call the Brave Dog Society. They talked about how they would dress, how they would use paint, what kind of rattles they would use, and how they would sit in a circle. They talked about who would become the leader, who would

---

1   Tipi rings refer to a circular pattern of rocks left on the ground, marking a place on the land where a tipi and tipi encampment once stood.

be the communicator, who could look after logistics, and who would be the members. All that organizational structure comes from an oral tradition. Each time they came together in circle, they sang the song for their society, and then Lone Chief gave that song to the old man, and he accepted it.

The [ceremony] went on all night, and then they had something to eat. And then the old man said, "Well, I'm going to go back to my camp. I've got to rest because I'm heading out to new camp" or what will become present camp. And then he left the old camp or Lone Chief's camp. He went across to his own lodge, and he fell asleep. And the next morning he woke up, and just the fire was there. There was no lodge. He was out in the open, and he was sleeping inside the rock circle of his tipi, but the dogs were all back. The pups and the female were all back by the fire. So, anyway, he picked up what he needed. He picked up the pups, and then he started hauling them back from old camp. The female followed all the way back to "new" becoming "present-day" camp. As he was walking back to this camp, he heard these brave dogs singing their song. He then realized that he had put the pups in a bag and thrown them over his back. They were singing. He listened and learned those songs all the way back. He finally got to the new "present-day" camp, and everybody came back out. They said, "Somebody's coming into camp." So the scouts came out, and here they recognized "That's the old man who was here and left already." So they were glad to see him. And he said, "Don't touch me, because I went through a transformation."

Lone Chief was actually a dog, and the young people in this camp were all dogs, and he told his people, "They transferred to me the strategic plan for the Brave Dog Society. So now I'm a member of the Brave Dog Society. You can't touch me. You need to build a sweat lodge for me. Once I have come out of the sweat, you can touch me." He said, "The young people in camp have to build the lodge for me." So the scouts went back, and they brought all the young people out, and they built a sweat lodge for him, and he started telling them the story. He started transferring to the leadership of the Brave Dog Society. He organized them all into that framework, and then they prepared a sweat lodge for him. He went in, and the leaders went in with him. He transferred the society framework to them, and then they became Brave Dogs. So, every time they make a sweat lodge or a smudge inside a camp, the leader of Brave Dogs would say, "Okay, I'm making this smudge. I'm transforming all of you into dogs. You're all related. You are all *relatives now: grandparents, older brothers, younger sisters, and so on. In this circle, you become the Brave Dog Society relatives."*

He shared this new framework with the rest of the camp, and other young people wanted to join this new society. So, when they were planning for new camp, and how to get to the new camp, they said, "We'll have an extra society that's going to help all the old people move." So, when I thought of that story, the old camp was where we looked for stories [when developing the University of Calgary Indigenous Strategy]. We consulted with everybody, and we met with the Elders and the university. So that was the knowledge that old Chief had. Before he was inviting this old man, he was collecting all those stories. When he brought the stories to present-day camp, he said, "Don't touch me until I go through a ceremony of bringing home the stories." When you bring home the stories, you have to analyze them. And, as he was analyzing them, that's when he made the framework for the new society to follow and transform into. And the seasons were part of that group. So then there was an annual visitation to that ceremony so that they can have it four times.

And that's how they moved to present-day camp. But they're using that as a framework for new camp when we're planning for new camp. So, when we say we're going to always be in transition, that means we're always going to be moving to new camp. We need to develop these [frameworks] at present-day camp and practise them as we [transform]. . . . Then they [frameworks] will work for new camp. So that was going back to an oral narrative of how we would look at oral systems of building strategies and transforming people to move ahead. But, at the same time, the environment and life exist all the time. It's going to be rotating all the time. And that new camp is always in that future rotation. You'll be always working toward it.

Oral Teaching, Piikani Elder Dr. Reg Crowshoe

Setting Out

Dru Marshall, Reg Crowshoe, Jacqueline Ottmann

2

Four Stories

PARALLEL PRACTICES

If we're going to develop a strategy with a framework to transform, then we have to go back to those oral narratives that the Elders hold. And then, when we know each other, we can achieve the goals we need to achieve, especially today when we're talking about reconciliation. From that knowledge from my father, Aapohsoy'yiis [Weasel Tail],[2] in our language, the concept of parallels in practice was instilled in my mind. My father instilled parallels along with the understanding of the wampum belt. I would say we achieved this. We followed that ecosystem of that river to survive together. But the practices need to parallel each other. We can't intertwine, or we're going to get cultural confusion, and we're going to crash our boats, and we'll never survive.

Reg Crowshoe

RELATIONAL VERSUS TRANSACTIONAL

One of my main lessons from the process to develop the Indigenous Strategy is how important it is to be relational rather than transactional. If we were more relational as a university with everything that we did, then we would be better. If you start from "How can I get to know you better?" then you will have a better understanding of where people are coming from—which should lead to making better decisions together.

Dru Marshall

---

2   Aapohsoy'yiis was a Peigan-Blackfoot Elder; see Crowshoe (2008).

COMMITMENT AND RISK

Setting out required a higher level of commitment for all involved. The non-Indigenous members of the Steering Committee and Working Group had to commit to learning Indigenous histories, traditions, practices, stories, and ceremonies and to surrender, to varying degrees, the comfort and familiarity of Eurocentric systems and structures to meet Indigenous peoples in the middle. This is analogous to the bridge created by the hand-shake between the two leaders, Indigenous and non-Indigenous, on treaty medallions. We were in this unique space. Indigenous peoples have had to code-talk, be culture brokers, conform to dominant ways to survive, but this Indigenous Strategy process had non-Indigenous people who engaged in learning; they crossed the floor so that we could co-create, co-plan, and experience reciprocal, respectful, and restorative relations through the creation of this plan. There was risk involved since we were setting out into uncertain and unknown territory. This was the first Indigenous Strategy for the university, and it was exhilarating to be a part of history in the making.

Jacqueline Ottmann

JOURNEY FRAMEWORK

Early on, we had a conversation with Elder Reg Crowshoe to develop a journey framework that reflected concepts of a group of people coming together on a quest to seek out and bring back resources to help sustain the community. The four-stage journey evolved from that concept. The Calling Together and Setting Out stage was about coming together as a group. Clearing the Path and Gathering Stories was about listening, learning, and capturing stories. Bringing the Stories Home was a process of making meaning, leading to the conceptualization of the strategy. Empowering the Spirit of Indigenization focused on ceremonial validation, institutional approval, and community celebration. A series of ceremonies guided our journey. When I reflect on our journey, I feel like we were immersed in ceremonial ways of doing. Our journey was enriched by ceremony. It was truly transformational, individually and collectively.

Shawna Cunningham

Creating Parallel Pathways

For many years, the University of Calgary benefited from established partnerships, collaborations, and education programs with Indigenous communities, organizations, and students in scholarly research and academic programming. However, none of these initiatives were developed with a specific institutional strategy in place for engaging Indigenous communities. Nor were these relationships developed from a foundation that fully acknowledged and honoured Indigenous peoples' histories, lived realities, sophisticated ways of knowing, and rich cultural practices. As a result, our relationships with Indigenous communities were scattered across the institution, taking many forms and varying in the depth and quality of the relationship. The development of an Indigenous Strategy therefore demanded the creation of new pathways for the institution and its relationships.

As one might expect, the university had well-developed frameworks—procedures and processes of approval—to develop new institutional strategies. These frameworks had been refined in the years leading up to the start of developing a new Indigenous Strategy. During an exciting time for the institution, new strategies such as the International Strategy, Mental Health Strategy, and Sustainability Strategy had been developed and approved. The first steps in developing an Indigenous Strategy followed these established processes. To begin the institutional Indigenous Strategy, leadership was identified, relevant committees were conceptualized, committee memberships started to take form, and a road map for institutional reviews and approvals was confirmed.

In creating and launching its Indigenous Strategy, the University of Calgary made a fundamental commitment. That commitment was to pursue a process of reconciliation that would genuinely honour Indigenous peoples' histories, worldviews, stories, knowledges, traditions, and lived experiences. A core aspect of this commitment was to reset, restore, and renew authentic relationships with Indigenous peoples and communities. Doing so would require the entire university community, and particularly those tasked with developing the strategy, to engage in proactive, deep learning. This journey would require cultural humility, extensive guidance by Traditional Knowledge Keepers, and trust in the new and unfamiliar process. This strategic process also demanded that Indigenous ceremonial approaches be considered as important as dominant decision-making processes typically used within postsecondary systems.

Based on this commitment to reconciliation, it was quickly evident that the creation of an Indigenous Strategy had to be very different from previous university strategy processes. Both approaches—a well-established university-based strategy process and Indigenous ways of knowing and decision making—needed to be honoured and adopted. It was also clear that neither approach could dominate the other, for doing so would undoubtedly lead to the assimilation of concepts, ideas, and practices. Based on the history of relationships with Indigenous peoples in Canada, a strictly institutional approach ran the risk of replicating and perpetuating colonizing structures and practices. So it was decided that parallel pathways had to guide the strategy. Rather than trying to "blend" frameworks based on significantly different worldviews, dual Eurocentric and Indigenous pathways were pursued concurrently. It was essential to create an approach that uplifted and supported both frameworks. Moreover, our chosen parallel path to develop the Indigenous strategy was uncertain and demanded extensive dialogue and constant reflection to align the work.

Interestingly, this parallel process followed the vision of relationships and political agreements between Indigenous peoples and non-Indigenous people as intended in treaty agreements such as the first treaty between the Haudenosaunee and the Dutch in 1613. As with the Two Row Wampum—Gaswéñdah,[3] creation of the Indigenous Strategy needed to engage the principles of peace, friendship, and trust as we moved through the process.

For every step of the journey, we needed to ensure that the two often competing worldviews were held in balance, not interfering with or dominating each other, but moving toward a common vision in parallel.

Indigenous Strategy Task Force

STEERING COMMITTEE

A Steering Committee was established to guide development of the Indigenous Strategy, facilitate dialogue between the University of Calgary

---

3   For the history of the Two Row Wampum—Gaswéñdah, see Onondaga Nation (2024).

and several Indigenous communities (including First Nations, Inuit, and Métis), and ensure that the strategy was ready for approval by the appropriate bodies. The Steering Committee was led by two co-chairs, including a senior university leader (the provost and vice-president academic) and a leading Indigenous scholar and director of Indigenous Initiatives from the Werklund School of Education. Other members of the Steering Committee included academic and administrative leaders from across the campus and several Traditional Knowledge Keepers. Co-chairs of the Working Group were also included in this membership.

The thirteen members of the Steering Committee were selected for their specific knowledge and expertise and expected to participate fully in the process of creating the strategy. This included responding collectively to the initial direction set by the university, articulating principles underlying the work, developing parallel governance processes, and advocating the strategy in the university and Indigenous communities. Members of this committee also committed to gaining a better understanding of the histories, lived experiences, cultures, identities, and interests of Indigenous peoples and to acquire a wider knowledge of diverse Indigenous ways in areas related to leadership, governance, pedagogy, decision making, and ethical spaces.

WORKING GROUP

The Working Group reported to and took direction from the Steering Committee. It was tasked with planning and completing the concrete steps required for consultations in the process of developing the strategy, compiling information relevant to the strategy, and writing drafts of the strategy document. This included conducting a broad review of external and internal programs, policies, initiatives, and protocols related to Indigenous Strategies. The Working Group was led by two co-chairs, a senior academic leader (the dean of the Faculty of Social Work) and a senior Indigenous leader (the long-standing director of the Native Centre). The Working Group comprised thirty-seven individuals, including faculty members from across the university, staff members and leaders from multiple administrative units, student leaders, and Indigenous community representatives, with cultural and spiritual guidance from Traditional Knowledge Keeper and Piikani Elder Dr. Reg Crowshoe.

The Working Group's efforts were to be supported by external literature and research and by the knowledge and practices of Indigenous communities embodying traditional cultures and lifestyles. For that purpose, members of the Working Group were asked to identify the cultural and environmental factors at the University of Calgary that would contribute to an Indigenous Strategy and to summarize the Indigenous research at the university.

First Steps

From the established strategy processes of the university, a series of necessary steps was identified and implemented. As the Steering Committee and Working Group were being created, terms of reference were written to articulate the "standard" institutional process for development of the strategy, which included defined leadership and accountability assigned to the appointed Steering Committee and Working Group. These terms followed typical lines of institutional accountability and reporting. They also reinforced the multiple approvals that would be required to adopt the Indigenous Strategy once it was completed. The institutional process therefore commenced with the appointment of the Indigenous Task Force, including co-chairs and members of a smaller Steering Committee and larger Working Group.

The co-chairs of the Steering Committee and Working Group worked to identify and add members of each group, paying close attention to ensuring broad representation from across the university's constituent groups. For the Steering Committee, this included members of the university's senior leadership team representing areas such as student services, government relations, and multiple faculties.

Three Traditional Knowledge Keepers were added to the Steering Committee and served as critical advisers and cultural guides in developing the Indigenous Strategy. For the Working Group—typically made up of various representatives from across the campus—invitations were extended to several Indigenous representatives from key community organizations with specific areas of interest and expertise in the development of strategies. The inclusion of Indigenous community voices in the Working Group and Traditional Knowledge Keepers in the Steering Committee marked a departure from the typical institutional process of developing strategies, introducing and shaping a new, albeit culturally parallel, way of doing for the university, and it was crucial to the creation of our Indigenous Strategy.

SETTING OUT

Led and facilitated by the Steering Committee and Working Group, the University of Calgary implemented a work plan that included a consultation framework to help guide the path, inform the content, and shape the creation of the Indigenous Strategy. Although the established terms of reference outlined a typical process for developing strategies at the institution, discussion in the Steering Committee quickly made it clear that another process would be required to honour Indigenous ways of knowing and doing. Based on this, the development of an Indigenous Strategy for the University of Calgary undoubtedly required the development of two parallel frameworks:

1. an institutional framework governed by the university's "Terms of Reference" document; and

2. an Indigenous framework guided by a parallel Indigenous document titled *Journey towards an Indigenous Strategy*, outlining a four-stage journey framework.

The university viewed working within the context of the two distinct yet parallel frameworks as a valuable and necessary developmental process for the Indigenous Strategy. For the Steering Committee and Working Group members, understanding of and commitment to the parallel framework were imperative. In one of the early Steering Committee meetings, one of the members voiced that the Indigenous Strategy needed a drastically different process, one that relied on Indigenous ways of knowing and doing. This realization progressed to the recognition of two parallel pathways by Elders in the group, especially Elders Reg Crowshoe [Áwákaasiina] from Piikani, Evelyn Goodstriker from Standing Buffalo, and Roy Weasel Fat from Kainai, and ceremonial leader Andy Black Water [Aa tso towa], also from Kainai. In addition, with a broadly defined vested stakeholder group that included internal and external communities, community engagement throughout the developmental process was deemed an essential part of the journey.

The initial timeline proposed for development and completion of the Indigenous Strategy was set between March and December 2016. Within weeks of this determination, however, members of the Working Group realized that the process demanded a longer timeline to ensure that mutual understanding of worldviews and processes was respected and accommodated. This was emphasized by the Traditional Knowledge Keepers and Indigenous leaders within the group. There was significant learning to be achieved, and creating the strategy required building authentic relationships based on trust, particularly with Indigenous communities. Adopting a parallel Indigenous framework also recognized the importance of ceremony and Indigenous decision-making processes. As a result, our timeline for completion of the strategy was extended from an initial six months to two years. The public launch of the University of Calgary's Indigenous Strategy occurred in November 2017.

PARALLEL STRATEGY FRAMEWORKS

Whereas the terms of reference for the provost's Task Force laid out a standard institutional process for development of the strategy, a parallel Indigenous framework did not exist. We knew that it had to be unique to the University of Calgary, and the resulting framework was designed through extensive consultation and reflection with Traditional Knowledge Keepers. It articulated the path to an inaugural Indigenous Strategy within the context of a four-stage evolutionary journey. These stages focused on the wisdom and collection of stories from Indigenous worldviews. The four stages, listed below and described extensively in later chapters, were validated by the Steering Committee and through ceremony conducted by Traditional Knowledge Keepers.

It is important to note that the Indigenous framework, titled *Journey towards the Indigenous Strategy*, was designed to follow essential Indigenous processes. It was seen as a journey in which challenges and tensions encountered along the way would be brought into the circle to have dialogue, seek advice, and in many cases request and receive ceremonial guidance from the Elders. It was also a framework in which progress and milestones were celebrated and validated through ceremony.

The Indigenous journey framework comprised the following four stages: (1) Calling Together and Setting Out, (2) Gathering Stories and

Clearing the Path, (3) Bringing the Stories Home, and (4) Empowering the Spirit of Indigenization. Each stage paralleled a stage conceptualized through the Eurocentric, institutional framework (University of Calgary 2017b, 40).

Table 1
Journey toward an Indigenous Strategy: Two Parallel Frameworks

	Institutional Framework (Written Terms of Reference)	Indigenous Framework (Oral Collection of Stories)
Stage 1	Developing Terms of Reference Setting Goals Confirming Committee Membership	Calling Together and Setting Out: Defining a Common Purpose
Stage 2	Information Gathering Data Collection	Clearing the Path and Gathering Stories
Stage 3	Data Compilation and Analysis	Bringing the Stories Home
Stage 4	Strategy Writing Approvals and Launch	Empowering the Spirit of Indigenization

The creation of these parallel pathways became both a defining element of the Indigenous Strategy and a deeply felt responsibility among members of the Working Group and Steering Committee. There were several points in the journey where the committees paused to reflect on our progress, consider key challenges, and imagine next steps. Throughout the process, members of these groups found that aligning these parallel pathways created a vibrant and rewarding experience, one that consistently added energy, direction, and purpose to the process.

TOUCHSTONES FOR OUR JOURNEY

With parallel frameworks developed to guide the Indigenous Strategy, members of the Steering Committee and Working Group engaged with Knowledge Keepers to better understand the touchstones of the process ahead. There were many conversations about the nature of this strategy, the journey itself, and how to ensure the meaningful inclusion of Indigenous voices. Particularly in the early stages, members of both groups expressed uncertainty and some anxiety about the profound responsibility that they felt to "get this right." Some non-Indigenous members felt inadequately prepared for the task and indicated that they did not know enough about Indigenous histories, lived experiences, and ways of knowing to help lead the effort. Other members said that they were not sure how an Indigenous Strategy would relate to their own areas of university life. Some were simply nervous about how they would be engaged in Indigenous ceremony. Although we all agreed that Indigenous voices needed to be central to the journey, many of us were unsure about how to best ensure that this was accomplished.

We found a critical driver to get past these initial concerns, and weeks of early inertia, was to engage in ongoing open and reflective dialogue in the scheduled meetings, gatherings, and ceremonies held for both groups. These dialogues identified some core epistemological and educational touchstones to be understood and revisited throughout our journey to continually ground and direct the strategy. According to Dr. Crowshoe, the idea of wayfinding draws from a Blackfoot/Piikani concept called *ii'yika'kimin*, which describes being guided by a spirit to choose a good direction and trying hard to follow this new path. Through such a spirit, these touchstones not only guided our journey but also distinguished this strategy from other institutional approaches to strategic development.

The first touchstone was rooted in inherent Indigenous governance, acknowledging the histories of Indigenous peoples in Canada. Colonial legislation, historical and current acts of racism, the genocide enacted by residential schools, and other efforts to assimilate or eradicate Indigenous Nations have shaped the relationships of Eurocentric institutions with Indigenous peoples. According to the *Final Report of the Truth and Reconciliation Commission of Canada* (TRC 2015), there remains a general lack of knowledge and understanding of Indigenous peoples' histories, rich and diverse cultures, complex belief systems, and practices among Canada's universities and the general population. This lack of knowledge and/or awareness—alongside a general lack of Indigenous representation in higher education overall—was confirmed during our consultations with our own campus community. Indigenous students are generally under-represented in postsecondary institutions across Canada, and historically universities have not been welcome learning environments for Indigenous students. Likewise, institutional research programs—most often founded upon Western principles and practices—typically have minimized and discounted Indigenous philosophies, pedagogies, and methodologies. In this context, Indigenous voices have been silenced, marginalized, and disregarded within the academy (Kuokkanen 2008). In the case of the University of Calgary, we needed to ensure that our Indigenous Strategy authentically recognized and served Indigenous peoples in both education and research.

Education has played a fundamental role in systemic racism, and the University of Calgary Indigenous Strategy Task Force quickly acknowledged that postsecondary institutions have a distinct responsibility to initiate and sustain reconciliation. Indeed, we felt a moral, ethical, and legal obligation to reset the university's relationship with Indigenous peoples. The institution needed to become genuinely inclusive and humble as we reimagined our processes of teaching, learning, and researching. This touchstone could be realized only through meaningful and reciprocal relationship building. It would also demand renewed "ways of being" for the university, deeply embedding "transformative reconciliation" (Burrows and Tully 2018) in the heart of the strategy.

A second touchstone was closely connected to the importance of including Indigenous people in the strategy as equal partners. Like most postsecondary institutions, the University of Calgary's historical connections to Indigenous communities were primarily transactional. These relationships were based on activities such as recruiting Indigenous students, providing basic supports as they experienced Eurocentric programs, and undertaking research driven by academic researchers' questions and methods. The Indigenous Strategy had to move beyond these transactional approaches, focusing instead on building deeper and more mutually beneficial relationships. The Indigenous Strategy Task Force recognized that this would be a long-term process, extending the timeline required for developing the strategy. Even as the process unfolded, members of the Steering Committee and Working Group spent considerable time with Elders and Knowledge Keepers, building the relationships required to understand the worldviews and practices necessary to make the strategy genuine.

A reconsideration of time represented another touchstone for the Steering Committee and Working Group. Most university strategies have limited time horizons, often about five years. It is expected that a strategy will be assessed and altered or renewed before the end of this time frame. Upon renewal, some strategies are replaced with new priorities. In developing the Indigenous Strategy, however, we realized that its inclusive and relational nature would demand commitments that extend far beyond typical institutional timelines. We came to consider the strategy as a generational document, a living entity that would continue to evolve for years and decades. This seemed to be both necessary and appropriate since the commitments made to long-term, authentic relationships with Indigenous communities could not have "end dates." We also realized that this principle mirrored the seventh-generation philosophy found in many Indigenous communities, where decision-making processes have stewardship at their core. Decisions made in the present must consider past learnings and ensure a sustainable environment seven generations into the future. In essence, we were planning not only for today but also for those children not yet born. We developed and implemented the University of Calgary Indigenous Strategy with these intentions at its core.

A final touchstone, the creation of ethical space, was also vital to the Indigenous Strategy. Ermine (2007, 193) describes a "space in between" Indigenous and Eurocentric worlds. The boundaries of this space are defined by distinct and vastly different worldviews, perspectives, cultures, and ways of being. Both Indigenous and Eurocentric worlds have undeniable rights and standing, meaning that they should relate with equal authority, status, and power. The colonization of Indigenous nations over recent centuries attempted to eliminate that standing, so developing genuine relationships demands restoration of that inherent equality.

Bridging worlds is a highly challenging task because the very assumptions and ways of communicating about the world are so distinct from one another. For example, Eurocentric ways of making decisions are founded upon written processes, formal organizational hierarchies, and procedures such as minuting and voting. In contrast, Indigenous decision-making processes are based on oral ways of knowing: ceremony, circular processes, responsibility that extends to ancestors and future generations, forms of consensus, and authorities based on tradition, responsibility, and transfer of rights. Historical processes of colonization imposed by dominant Eurocentric settlers, such as enforced assimilation and genocidal legislation, attempted to erase and silence Indigenous peoples' cultures, languages, practices, ceremonies, wisdom, and beliefs (TRC, 2015).

Eurocentric dominance, systemic racism, and the lingering colonial mindset is ever present. Cultural differences exist perpetually in the
overlapping space between worldviews and cultures, characterizing
the complexity, threatening the assimilation, and underscoring the fra-
gility of Indigenous and non-Indigenous relations. As noted, this space
in between two disparate cultures can be fraught with "jagged edges"
(Henderson 2009, 65). The collision of "jagged worldviews" (Little Bear
2000) can cause tension, conflict, or confusion. Between these edges is
also the potential to build an "ethical space of engagement" (Ermine 2007)
through dialogue and cultural parallels, creating a dynamic opportunity
for meaningful communication and sincere acknowledgement of the inherent sacredness of distinct worldviews. This "in between" space is full
of uncertainty and creativity and contains an innovative force; it is a place
where the courageous move past the familiar, untenable, and unworkable
to build something new. Addressing the colonial mindset and engaging
Indigenous communities in a more ethical and relational manner that acknowledges and honors Indigenous knowledge systems, lived experiences
and relational connection to land, calls for a framework of "ethical relationality" (Donald 2016).

The creation of ethical space became a touchstone for our journey
because developing an ethical relationship with Indigenous communities
demanded that the university fully acknowledge the devastating history
of colonization and its impacts on Indigenous peoples. We also needed
to recognize the role universities and other education systems played in
enforced assimilation practices of the Crown. Through legislated acts of
enfranchisement up to 1961, First Nations individuals who chose to better
themselves through higher education were forcefully enfranchised under
the Indian Act.[4] They lost their Indian Status, were stripped of their inherent Indigenous rights, and were forbidden to live in their First Nations
communities (Crey 2009). Once enfranchised, a First Nations person was
no longer recognized as an Indigenous person (Indian) under the Indian
Act and, by extension, the Canadian Constitution. We recognized the

---

4   Information about enfranchisement, the Gradual Enfranchisement Act, 1869, the
Gradual Civilization Act, 1857, and the Indian Act can be found at https://indigenousfoundations.
arts.ubc.ca/enfranchisement/.

historical context that would require us to address the history and aggressive acts of assimilation through education.

Creating ethical space to reimagine and reset trusted relationships with Indigenous communities would require the university to interact with Indigenous communities through *their* worldviews. We needed to become a place that embraced and engaged in deep learning about unique Indigenous worldviews, cultures, and practices. Guided by the spirit and actions embodied in these touchstones, the University of Calgary made several commitments in developing its Indigenous Strategy:

1. to engage in the process of reconciliation, which entails a collective journey that honours Indigenous peoples' stories, knowledges, and traditions, and the renewal and development of authentic relationships with Indigenous peoples and communities;

2. to establish a welcoming, inclusive, and culturally competent campus community that respects, includes, and promotes Indigenous ways of knowing, teaching, learning, and researching;

3. to create and maintain shared ethical space inclusive of Indigenous people's representation within the student body, staff, faculty, leadership, and governing structures;

4. to develop a campus community that understands the histories and worldviews of Indigenous peoples and the importance of connection to the land;

5. to ensure that policies, practices, and procedures are supportive and respectful of Indigenous ways;

6. to create spaces and processes for ongoing "full circle" community engagement through dialogue with Indigenous communities and other institutional stakeholders; and

7. to ensure sustainability and renewal of the Indigenous Strategy so that it remains a current and dynamic agent of transformation for the university. (See University of Calgary 2017b, 5)

The seven statements of commitment are grounded in an Indigenous epistemic axiology captured by the phrase "in a good way." This phrase signals ways of doing and being synonymous with concepts of relationality, enacted through a value system governed by respect and kindness for all our relations.

EMBRACING CULTURAL TEACHINGS

A foundational contribution from the Traditional Knowledge Keepers dialogue session held on November 18, 2016, was the emphasis on cultural teachings shared by a diverse group of Elders from several nations within the region. These teachings, derived from the common threads of Indigenous worldviews shared with us over the course of our journey, are at the heart of the Indigenous Strategy and include kindness, reciprocity, respect, relationality, interconnectedness, and collectivism. These cultural teachings guided our journey toward the development of our strategy, inspiring sharing and kindness rooted in a profound sense of responsibility to care for all our relations. Cornerstone practices such as meaningful engagement of communities, shared decision making, and inclusion of Indigenous pedagogies such as land-based learning, and the important role of Traditional Knowledge Keepers in course delivery, are integral to the call for reconciliation through education. Extending such thinking to the values and operating principles of a university could lead to profound transformation.

Transitional Story

PIPE BAG STORY

When I think about the pipe bag or any container in our culture, a container is something that we carry things in, and we protect them from getting lost or from losing them. So those are the thoughts I have when I talk about a pipe bag or a container. When I think about an organization coming together, the organization will have no need to become a society or an organization if they don't have anything common [that they carry with them]. But if they find a need in their community, then they would come together based on that need. And coming together they would have their discussion on what the need was.

Through that discussion, they [the organization] can prioritize all the important points that they brought up. And from the prioritized list, in Western culture, they'll write them down. And once they have them on a piece of paper, then that gives them their goals and objectives. That's how we understand the written system. But when you look at the oral system—with this pipe bag understanding—we also have shared goals and ideas and practices belonging to a group of people coming together for a [common] need, and through their discussion they prioritize that need.

However, in an oral culture, we didn't write, so what we did was, once we had the priorities, those priorities were represented with cultural items from an environment that we all share within all of creation, whether it's animals, plants, rocks, and so on. Those cultural items are brought together to represent those visions and missions. And of course we have to wrap them [the cultural items] up so they don't fall all over the place. So we have a pouch or a container. In a lot of cases, we'd say a pouch bag or a pipe bag [or a bundle] that we can put them in, and that's what we bring to all our meetings, so that represents our visions and mission.

We don't have Western practices. We don't have a file that we put in a filing cabinet, but what we do have is the bundle itself that's handed over through a ceremony, an oral practice, to somebody to be responsible for it. They'll know the knowledge. Usually the leader. Then, when the leader retires and a new leader comes in, that container is transferred to the new leader, and the old leader then becomes the keeper of our oral policies [our oral filing cabinet] to give us direction, advice, and help. That's why Elders are so important in the coming into circles of meetings.

Oral Teaching, Piikani Elder Dr. Reg Crowshoe

3

Coming into the Circle

Reg Crowshoe, Shawna Cunningham, Jackie Sieppert

Four Stories

TWO KNOWLEDGE SYSTEMS

I look at my father, Aapohsoy'yiisai [Weasel Tail], who wrote a story about his life titled Weasel Tail. He was born in 1898, 1899. When he was born, there were already residential schools. When he was sent to residential school, he was sent to residential school along the Old Man River near where he was born. It was called Victoria Home. So he would start talking about his experience—how transformation happened, how he had to follow the residential school, how he had to follow Indian Affairs policies throughout his life, and how the Indian Agent and the churches had so much power over him, and so on. And he would tell me, "Through all these experiences with the newcomers—their writing and their dominion—I know their system so good, I can become one of them." And then he would say, "However, if they knew my system, then they would know me. Then we can work together. But they don't know my system, and we're suffering all these years." So I think about that and say, "Yes, it's at the system level that we need to understand each other." We need to culturally interpret and translate at a practical level so we can understand. Weasel Tail said, "Through Western practice, I know what they do." So, based on that knowledge from Weasel Tail, I say it's that practical knowledge that we have to culturally translate and culturally interpret system languages so that we know the practices so well, so we can know each other. And then, when we know each other, we can achieve the goals we need to achieve. Especially today when we're talking about reconciliation. From that knowledge that came from my father, in our language, the concept of parallels in practice was instilled in my mind in my young years. Weasel Tail's teaching helped me to find those parallels in practice.

Reg Crowshoe

CIRCLES AND LINES

For us, the first creation was number one. The symbol for number one is the Sun, number two is the Moon, number three is Morning Star, and number four is Scarface. Anyway, I knew that, and I can count in an Indigenous way. However, when I went to residential school, I wasn't allowed to speak my language. And there we got different symbols for counting or numeration, I guess we call it. As much as we couldn't speak our language, we couldn't use our Blackfoot symbols either. In residential school, we were taught that a line was the symbol for number one. And in my young mind, I was confused, but I didn't want to speak up. But I knew that the circle, in our way, was the symbol for the sun, and the sun is number one. So Western knowledge was superimposing the line over the circle. That was my confusion. When I went home, I told my Grandmother that story of different symbols for the number one—the circle and the line—and my challenge in understanding the symbol of the line versus the circle. My Grandmother straightened it out for me. She said, "Creator gave us all our different languages and dialects, even in symbols. The circle is right. Creator gave us that to be the symbol for the sun. But he also gave the other people [Western people] the [straight] line up and down. They both mean the same thing. You can use both." I always go back to the old lady's (my Grandmother's) words. When I look at the idea of imposing one over the other, I look at it as cultural confusion. And cultural confusion is alive today, especially when organizations say "We want to intertwine the two distinct cultural ways of knowing or combine Indigenous cultures with 'written' cultures."

Reg Crowshoe

KIMMAPIIPITSINI: SANCTIFIED KINDNESS

To me, sanctified kindness is an interpretation of kimmapiipitsini *(to be kind). It's that humility and humbleness to remember that we (all those in creation) are equal so that we can safely survive together. And I guess that's where kindness comes in, where we take that humility and even the responsibility of kindness, so that we can be kind to everything. If I wasn't kind to the sweetgrass, and I didn't look after the sweetgrass as part of my responsibility, then the sweetgrass is going to disappear from creation. And when it does, then how are we going to use sweetgrass in our smudge as a call to order? So that would be the concept of kindness—when we sanctify kindness for all. When we "call to order" and make the smudge, we consider all of creation. This comes from the concept of natural laws where, as my Grandmother taught me, "All creation respects and is kind to each other, and that's how we learn to then be kind to ourselves." And the other important thing that I learned, as an oral concept, is that, when I have an idea (or a thought), I have to bring it through a smudge process to make it real. I think in Western practice you might refer to that as developing a policy. It's a thought, and you bring it through a process, and that process gives you direction. So, when I come up with a thought, sanctified kindness has got to be a part of it, because I've got to bring that kindness to the gathering, to the smudge—because the gathering is the process to validate or to make my thought real. That's the process of sanctified kindness. I bring my thoughts to the gathering, and then we all have the input into it and validate it as an idea. Then it becomes real. It becomes validated by the venue and the smudge. Through the smudge and sanctified kindness, I have to consider all my people or all my relatives in the environment so that I'm not harming them. The process of sanctified kindness must give us all survival. It's my responsibility to natural laws to make things real. That's how I view sanctified kindness.*

Reg Crowshoe

TRANSFORMATION THROUGH THE SMUDGED CIRCLE

When I went into the Little Birds, the Elder made a smudge to initiate a "call to order." At the same time, however, she said, "All right, all of you sitting in this circle are all transformed into Little Birds. You're all Little Birds. When we made the smudge, we transformed you." So as soon as that happened with the smudge, we all became equal. We weren't children from different families. We weren't children from different parts of the reserve. We were all equal as Little Birds. With the Little Birds, we had four stories to introduce. The four stories were a part of all those circles as I grew up. We had progressive levels of learning or circles. Each time we went to another level, we were told four stories, or we shared four stories. Those four stories were alignment or concept stories that prepared us to go to the next level. And throughout all the circles, whether it's the Bumble Bees, the Brave Dogs, the Thunder Pipes, the other societies, the four stories are an important concept to set direction through alignment but also through a concept of how we're going to work within a framework of some sort, how we're going to achieve our goals based on the four stories given or offered. So I relate those four stories to a parallel in written systems that talk about building strategies and a framework for a strategy, because we develop a concept that allows us to build a Western written framework or strategies, say to transform or whatever. Those are four concepts that are important. So that's how I relate the four stories in our circle. So we've got the smudge to "call us to order," we've got the circle as a venue, we've got the four concepts to give us the framework of what we're going to enter and what we're going to do.

Reg Crowshoe

Our Parallel Journey

The Indigenous Strategy *ii' taa'poh'to'p* was informed and enriched by consultations, conversations, and ceremonial guidance from many Traditional Knowledge Keepers identified in the Indigenous Strategy document (University of Calgary 2017b, 50). Traditional Knowledge Keepers became an important part of our journey. The creation of the strategy was part of a parallel practice that engaged in ceremonial validation, transfers, and blessings associated with a four-stage journey framework that felt right for the University of Calgary. The parallel practice adopted an oral concept of becoming relatives to inform a collective, collaborative, and ethical space in which to achieve a common purpose. Reg Crowshoe explains the foundation of this parallel approach:

> When I talk to organizations about transformation, or a framework to help develop a strategy of transformation, I always go back to the system of building relatives. We become real to each other when we are relatives. Through this process, we work together so that everyone can survive rather than creating something we must conform to. So it's not building relatives to make people conform to something but to work collectively to transform organizations in a way that we all can survive together. You're putting another option out there, an oral system's option where we are transforming through making relatives rather than mere policies. System change through Western policy creates fear and resistance in the organization. You don't want to be looking at organizational change where people are going to ask, "Why do I have to?" This type of system change creates resistance. So why not use the option of building relatives as a "buy-in" to a system of survival where we work together in achieving a goal? So that's how, through my knowledge system, I thought about how to create a framework to work with the whole institution, the University of Calgary. I thought "We need to work with an Indigenous framework based on building relatives."

This chapter provides an overview of the key cultural teachings that helped to ground, shape, and guide the development of the University of Calgary Indigenous Strategy. To fully capture and disseminate the story of *ii' taa'poh'to'p*, we wove traditional knowledge into the chapter via a series of conversational interviews with Piikani Elder Dr. Reg Crowshoe [Áwákaasiina/Deer Chief]. He was a key member of the Steering Committee, helping to guide our journey through parallel cultural practices and teachings now embedded in *ii' taa'poh'to'p*. Crowshoe imparted key cultural teachings that reflect a Piikani worldview based on oral transfers grounded in intergenerational knowledge and validated through venue, action, language, and song. This knowledge is interpreted and evoked through lived experiences and traditional oral practices.

Co-creation of the Indigenous Strategy involved walking two parallel paths. The generous teachings from Traditional Knowledge Keepers are embedded in the strategy's unique content and structure, honouring Indigenous ways of knowing. Our parallel path was a journey of evolutionary transformation for the individuals involved, inspiring the University of Calgary to take up the call for reconciliation as guided by *ii' taa'poh'to'p*. Developing the strategy required a mindful and sustainable approach that included space to explore, reflect, and engage fully and meaningfully with community. The process was cyclical rather than linear, and the work was inherently relational. The initial phase of the work, reflected in this chapter, involved moving through trepidation, ambiguity, and anxiety to arrive at a new place of understanding and commitment for all involved in the journey. It was a process of "coming into the circle," creating a common purpose, and taking the first steps toward truth and reconciliation. The journey was enriched and affirmed by Indigenous worldviews and methods as core to the process and experience. In this chapter, we share some of the foundational cultural teachings and onto-epistemological frameworks that shaped the coming into the circle aspect of our developmental journey.

Coming into the Circle

The cycle of life is a process, derived from the natural laws of the universe, that encompasses concepts of circularity. Conceptual circles shape a core understanding of the world and the practices that flow from that understanding. Many Indigenous cultures have adopted practices to reflect circularity in nature, including ceremonial practices, concepts of time, communal structures, decision-making processes, and architectural designs such as tipis. Below is a reflective conversation with Reg Crowshoe:

> Jackie Sieppert: The book is going to start with the notion of coming into the circle. And part of that, for us, is about the teaching associated with the four stories. So we wanted to start there and ask if you could explain the teachings associated with the offering of four stories.

> Reg Crowshoe: When I think about the circle, to us everything is in a circle. The whole life is in the cycle, a life cycle. The circle itself—we see it in four directions or four circles, also counting to four, or in our creation stories. The knowledge of four gives us that practice of a circle. We sit in a circle, stand in a circle, and dance in a circle. Our tipis are in circles, life is in circles; it gives us the practice of a circle.
>
> I think the way I look at the four stories is that the four stories were created as individuals would come into the circle. When we come into the circle, and the leader asks for four stories, the four stories are an oral narrative of a creation. This is a process of knowledge creation. The practice of creation happens when someone brings in a thought, idea, or truth. This form of truthing represents an invisible infrastructure where there are consequences if we do something wrong. That concept of creation is what we call a power, a jurisdiction, a spirit. So, if we do something bad against this creation, like in all creation, I and my relatives suffer the consequence. That's an important understanding of the creation of those four stories. Then we go to the physical part to say the four stories will talk about how that creation came together and the storied experience of individuals. The narrative or research from that experience becomes the physical representation of what is real to us. So the four stories represent a real concept or event that happened. I would look at the stories as jurisdiction. It's a form of truthing, so it has jurisdiction or authority. So, when you bring the story into a process like decision making or transfer of knowledge, that is part of your jurisdiction going

into the process for making decisions. A lot of Elders speak about it [truthing through story] as a spirit. When you bring the story into the circle, the spirit comes with it, so automatically there's a jurisdiction evoked.

Foundational Cultural Teachings

The development of the Indigenous Strategy was grounded in cultural teachings guided by the concepts of parallel paths, sanctified kindness, and ethical space that helped us to move forward "in a good way." These concepts, together with reflections on the journey, and related learnings, are presented through stories and conversational sections.

For many Indigenous peoples, oral knowledge and worldviews are accessed through language, action, venue, and song,[1] often in the context of ceremony. Complex epistemologies are best expressed and/or understood within the language of origin. In a traditional context, Elders recognized by the community are the keepers of the knowledge, with rights of expression, dissemination, and transfer bestowed through oral practices such as ceremony. For the most part, Indigenous knowledge is held, protected, and articulated within the construct of the language and the intergenerational oral practices therein. Knowledge acquisition, preservation, and dissemination are based on an enduring, relational, and fundamental understanding of the world, grounded by natural laws and cyclical universal principles of living with and within an inextricably interconnected "living" and ever-evolving ecosystem. In that sense, everything in creation is interactive, responsive, and constantly in communication with universal circular patterns found in nature. There is a highly sensory dimension to creation.

In this light, Indigenous knowledge is based on oral traditions and practices rather than the standardized confines of written knowledge that dominate colonial education systems, based on a foundation of what L'nu Mi'kmaq scholar Marie Battiste (2013, 26) calls "cognitive imperialism," by which "a Eurocentric foundation is advanced to the exclusion of other knowledges and languages." Oral knowledge, most traditionally, was and still is accessed through language or the Traditional Knowledge

---

1   Oral teaching from Reg Crowshoe, January 17, 2023.

Keeper. Most often Indigenous knowledge is based on enduring and fundamental understanding that the world, and all within it are relationally interconnected and cyclical in nature. In that sense, everything is part of a perpetual and relational circular motion, evolving through dynamic spirals emanating from the natural laws of the universe, in sync with and engaged in "universal flux" (Little Bear 2000, 85), the ebb and flow of all life, the pulse of all creation.

IN A GOOD WAY

The following is an excerpt from the Indigenous Strategy document *ii' taa'poh'to'p*:

> *In a good way* is a concept used by many Indigenous peoples to recognize work that is conducted in authentic and meaningful ways, with intention and sincerity, through reciprocal and respectful relationships. It is a demonstration of working with clear purpose and with high levels of integrity, moral strength, and communal spirit. The guiding principle for the Indigenous Strategy therefore starts with the commitment to work together with Indigenous communities "in a good way."
>
> The journey toward an Indigenous Strategy is one that involves deep change at the University of Calgary. This change is evolutionary. It will require ongoing dialogue with Indigenous communities, thoughtful reflection, building upon successes, and changing the general university narrative over time. It is inherently a process of long-term relationship building. The realization of the Strategy will require patience and dedication, as reconciliation will be an ongoing process for many years—perhaps generations. Based on this, another foundational element in the guiding principle is the Indigenous focus on transformation and renewal, a dynamic universal cycle based on natural laws of change, adaptation, and evolution. (University of Calgary 2017b, 13)

In addition to the guiding principle of working in a good way, the following concepts reflect the processes of change built into the foundation of this Indigenous Strategy.

PARALLEL PATHS

Choosing to walk a path toward reconciliation represents a generational commitment based on a foundation of compassion, cross-cultural learning, and humility. It brings tremendous responsibility to commit to building new knowledge and deeply understand Indigenous perspectives, worldviews, histories, cultures, and belief systems. It also demands the ability to interrogate the dominant worldviews, structures, and processes that oppress Indigenous peoples. Walking a path toward reconciliation requires establishing relationships that are mutually authentic, respectful, beneficial, and equal. The journey toward reconciliation therefore depends on creating parallel pathways in which no one particular worldview, knowledge, or way of doing dominates others. Canada's educational institutions share these responsibilities and must be leaders in creating the parallel pathways that will initiate and sustain reconciliation.

Because education played a fundamental part in the implementation of Canada's destructive policies of assimilation aimed at Indigenous peoples, the University of Calgary chose to acknowledge its moral and ethical obligations to walk the path toward reconciliation. The university committed to renewing relationships with Indigenous peoples and to creating an inclusive, mindful, and respectful teaching, learning, and research institution.

Those tasked with developing the University of Calgary's Indigenous Strategy felt this daunting obligation to develop a parallel process. Success would demand new understanding, knowledge, and commitment, in fact a new form of postsecondary strategy development. We knew that the process needed to reflect mandated university governance structures and procedures, including broad institutional consultations, committee processes, and levels of institutional approval. Such processes are inherently based on the historical, written language traditions of postsecondary systems. They result in textual documents such as committee terms of reference, various reports, and an Indigenous Strategy to be presented in written form.

Throughout our journey, Indigenous knowledge systems needed to be given equal standing with historical university processes. The knowledge shared by and the guidance received from Traditional Knowledge Keepers were fundamental to our process as well as the final strategy document. Engagement in ceremonial ways of doing (oral practices) was transformative for individuals involved in the developmental journey. Giving oral and written practices equal standing throughout the journey changed the nature of the strategy and has become synonymous with the story of the university.

The development of the university's Indigenous Strategy therefore embraced two distinct worldviews, neither of which overshadowed the other. One of the teachings shared by Reg Crowshoe originated with his Grandmother, Iikia'yisst siiyi oh'paa'ta [All Listens For], who addressed concepts of what we now recognize as the colonization and contamination of Indigenous knowledge systems. The teachings shared by his Grandmother were passed down to Reg as uncontaminated knowledge in the old Blackfoot language, free from Western interference and acts of colonization:

> We can't intertwine the two worldviews, or we'll get cultural confusion. My Grandmother would say "Creator gave the written system and the oral system as administrative practices to each culture." So they're both equal. Oral practices such as a traditional song [like treaty songs] are an administrative practice that is equal to written documents [like the written treaties]. We must acknowledge oral practices as equally valid knowledge systems—like the Mohawk's use of the wampum belt or the metaphorical concept of two canoes on a river, travelling in the same direction but not crossing, bumping, or crashing into each other. And if we can do that, then we can work together.

Based on this understanding, the resulting process to develop the Indigenous Strategy was iterative and cyclical. Recognizing and respecting multiple and diverse worldviews and ways of knowing became essential. Although we understood the university's dominant processes, non-Indigenous participants had limited understanding of Indigenous

Final Pipe Ceremony. June 21, 2017. University of Calgary. Photo Credit: Riley Brandt, UCalgary.

ways of knowing. We needed to pause routinely to develop understanding, seek guidance from Traditional Knowledge Keepers, and choose practices that reflected an authentic commitment to this parallel path. Such a path had to be grounded in ceremony, and those developing the strategy had to engage in deep learning that often challenged existing values and belief systems, assumptions, and routine practices.

A core challenge in creating this parallel path was ensuring alignment between written and oral practices. For example, many individuals in the Working Group, particularly non-Indigenous institutional appointees, had never participated in an Indigenous ceremony and were apprehensive at first. However, once they became accustomed to the repetitive practice of smudging and taking part in pipe ceremonies throughout the journey, they embraced the safety and belonging that the ceremonies provided. Staying true to this parallel path beyond the Working Group and Steering Committee required constant, mindful attention. Dialogue among Traditional Knowledge Keepers, the Indigenous Task Force, and the rest of the institution was key. There were continual conversations about and cultural interpretations of the parallels between oral Indigenous and institutional, Eurocentric, written practices and structures.

In the spirit of co-creating the Indigenous Strategy, members of the Steering Committee and Working Group were guided by key cultural teachings from the Elders with whom we worked. These teachings ensured the inherent value and role of oral practices. One of the foundational teachings was about the importance of the circle and the smudge, as shared by Reg Crowshoe:

> The circle, the smudge, sanctified kindness, and the four stories (which give us alignment) are all oral practices that allow us to transfer knowledge or make decisions. Those oral practices or oral systems are similar to written practices. Western written practices have a place to make decisions, like a boardroom or classroom. They have their call to order, like the gavel. Therefore, oral stories, like the smudged four alignment stories, may be considered parallel to the directions set by written policy in Western systems. Those written policies are what I consider parallel to four stories or narratives that the Elders represent. Elders are our oral policies. So those are parallels in two systems. One is a written system, and one is an oral. In our oral system, there is system language. Part of my responsibilities and transparencies to natural laws is that we all survive together and sanctify kindness. So, when I think from that perspective, I think about creation. I think about . . . all different jurisdictions of different beings or relatives within creation.

SANCTIFIED KINDNESS (*KIMMAPIIPITSINI*)

Sanctified kindness is an interpretation of a Blackfoot concept named *kimmapiipitsini*. As a cultural concept, it is far broader than the concept of kindness commonly understood in the dominant culture. *Kimmapiipitsini* is grounded in the responsibility to be humble, to see all of creation as equal, to embody and extend kindness to everything around us—to all our relatives. However, it also reflects a collective responsibility to protect and honour natural laws—the source of survival. Relationships and collective processes require sanctified kindness to be real and respectful. One of Dr. Crowshoe's teachings articulates this profound responsibility:

All creations are natural law. That's what I call them, natural law. However, when they start interacting, there's many different types of interaction. . . . That interaction is creative by nature. So we say that interaction creates. For example, interaction between natural laws creates research; it creates an experience; it creates knowledge. And as it creates those narratives, they come to our circles as absolute laws. They come to our circles as knowledge. So those are the tools we use to be responsible and transparent to Creator, so that we all survive. So I look at the land and the ecosystem as a physical documentation of our laws. Like any other society around the world, we have laws, and we're responsible for them through our relationship within an ecosystem that we are all a part of.

It is perhaps this grounding in natural laws that most clearly separates the concept of sanctified kindness from the more limited understanding of kindness in the dominant worldview. Sanctified kindness embodies the iterative and dynamic interactions that connect all creation with the natural laws of our world—renewal, restoration, rejuvenation, relationship. It is more than the caring interactions among individuals, extending instead to the universal and circular connections noted in Little Bear's (2000) concept of "universal flux." In this sense, sanctified kindness is reflected in the ecosystems in which we are all a part, and it is essential to balance and survival.

ETHICAL SPACE

Willie Ermine (2007, 194) conceptualizes a dynamic space created between "Indigenous and Western thought worlds." The boundaries or parameters of this space are established through the human construction of firm and enduring conceptual models. These models, which define our cultural identities, establish understandings of the world, principles by which we live, and ways of interacting within and being in relations with the ecosystems of our environment. The differences between these "thought worlds" establish the uniqueness and diversity of Indigenous and Western communities based on distinct histories, knowledge traditions, philosophies, and social and political realities (Ermine 2007, 194).

Because Indigenous and Western thought worlds have such unique and often contrasting assumptions about and perceptions of the world, it is a challenge to easily communicate across the "space" that exists between them. Ermine (2007, 194) suggests that this reality has created "two solitudes" that must be bridged if reconciliation is to be experienced. This is particularly true given the extent to which the Western thought world has colonized the Indigenous thought world for centuries.

The idea of ethical space is based on the premise that Indigenous and Western thought worlds have inherent, inalienable rights and standing. There is a sacredness to these distinct thought worlds, and authentic relationships between them require a deep commitment to honouring and protecting the spirit inherent in each world. In essence, an ethical relationship between Indigenous and Western thought worlds requires the dominant culture to fully acknowledge and engage with Indigenous communities through their own histories, cultures, knowledge systems, and autonomous practices. People who espouse Western systems must recognize cognitive imperialistic acts and acknowledge historical and current transgressions against Indigenous communities and the mechanisms by which their thought world has violated the spaces within Indigenous communities.

Like Ermine (2007), Reg Crowshoe and David Lertzman (2020, 18) also suggest that, to realize ethical space, a mutual understanding must be established between Indigenous and Western perspectives on the environment and our place within it. This understanding must restore the trust and respect lost through the colonization of Indigenous peoples. Doing so will create safety in the relationship, one that allows for open, transparent communication. This, Crowshoe explains, is a critical and grounding component of ethical space:

> I look at any bio-ecosystem as one big ethical space. We need to survive together, and survival is the ethical space. . . . To avoid cultural confusion, we need to engage in survival with sanctified kindness and relatives, by allowing each individual to come into that space with their own worldview and responsibilities. We need to provide a safe space for the two individuals from disparate cultures to have a discussion, to understand each other. And that ethical space, it's just going

to be a space until you bring the two together and it comes alive; then it's ethical space. So that's the concept I look at as ethical space. The circle is our ethical space, the nest, the burrow, the beehive, and the mountain, where all those circles come from, those are giving us the basis of the circle, which is ethical space.

So, when I look at ethical space from a Western perspective and my understanding of Western practices, whatever the space is, a boardroom or a classroom, in order to make it safe, you need policies like codes of conduct and procedures, which allow two people to be able to talk about their opinions or share opposite opinions, but that's what makes it safe. So that's the ethical space. So I think about our classes, the circle when I was young, whoa, I think about that, and when I look at the walls of our tipi when I was young I always see the design. In our case, it was the *ii'kokaan* (lodge design), and I feel comfortable in my home looking at those designs. But if you look past those designs to the upper people—the stars, on the north side—we have the seven stars; the seven brothers give us procedure. So, when I make my smudge for sanctified kindness, the seven brothers and their stories, the seven learnings, gave us procedure as to how we do this in a safe space.

Ceremonial Ways of Doing

INVITATION INTO THE CIRCLE

A commitment to Indigenous ways of knowing and doing was essential to developing parallel pathways for the University of Calgary's Indigenous Strategy. One of these pathways was well understood within the university since it followed accepted governance procedures and practices. They included, for example, the use of committee structures, terms of reference, leadership assignments, and adherence to mechanisms of approval within the university governance structure. Such practices were an important part of the process to develop and approve the strategy.

However, development and validation of the strategy also demanded a parallel pathway that honoured and protected Indigenous governance systems. At every step, we needed to determine the parallel mechanism that would put Indigenous ways of knowing and doing on equal footing with the processes inherent to postsecondary institutions. Doing so necessitated constant conversations with Traditional Knowledge Keepers, working through ambiguity, and a willingness to defer or alter typical university processes. The process relied on understanding Indigenous oral practices in ways that most university personnel were not familiar with. Examples included smudging before meetings to open a safe and ethical space for respectful dialogue and meaningful decision making and honouring progress through cultural transfers and pipe ceremonies.

In this process, the concepts of circularity enacted in life and practice, along with the role of "alignment" stories, were critical to the development of an Indigenous Strategy. They became the starting point for coming into the circle with the primary purpose of making relatives and creating processes that affirmed Indigenous knowledge, governance procedures, and the essential role of ceremony. For the entire University of Calgary community, it required that we "live within the circle and think outside the box."[2]

THE SMUDGED CIRCLE

The concept of the smudged circle provides a powerful counterpart to executive decision making, boardroom procedures and rules, use of the gavel, and mechanisms affirming that a decision has been made. As Reg Crowshoe noted in a conversational interview in 2023,

> the smudge calls us to order, the circle is the venue, and the four stories/concepts give us the framework of what circle (or environment) we are going to enter and what we are going to do (or commit to doing). The smudge also constitutes a copyright; it is a framework and an introduction to the systems of truth telling and knowing that Indigenous worldviews are based on.

---

2   Gregory Cajete, personal communication with Jacqueline Ottmann, February 2014.

As a child, Reg was immersed in Blackfoot Knowledge and pedagogical practices through initiation into Blackfoot circle societies, the first being the Little Birds. Its circle or society, the first of many within his lifetime, represents a teaching and learning or pedagogical structure within a Blackfoot Piikani paradigm. As he reflected on the essential role of these societies, he said that,

> in Blackfoot culture, the bumble bees and their hives are represented in a circle, and the Brave Dog society has its own circle; so too do the Thunder Pipe societies, the Beaver Bundles societies, and the Sun Dance circle. So the circle has many meanings, but it all gives us the same practice of coming together in a common venue and purpose. The circle establishes a venue where we can develop a safe place to have a discussion, to learn, and to transfer knowledge through a call to order of the smudge within the circle.

The teachings imparted through the oral practices of this circle are comparable to, yet different from, the Western notion of a more formal, standardized curriculum. For the individual members and the collective cohort, the circular structures are progressive, building upon each other, a pedagogical model based on natural laws of the land, where belonging is a relational concept, encompassing all living beings and instilling a communal and "relational way of being" (Wilson 2008) through a process of what Crowshoe calls "making relatives." Teachings are shared and understood through a communal and relational lens of respectful reciprocity specific to the land and the Indigenous ancestral community from which they are drawn.

MAKING RELATIVES

According to Reg Crowshoe in an oral teaching shared in 2023, "when we acknowledge the land as a relative when we are sitting in circle, we must ask ourselves: how does that land acknowledgement connect us to the natural laws of the land?" He shared that the "smudge honours the land. Land is a physical representation of our natural laws. Therefore, a land acknowledgement recognizes that our society has governance and laws—and that circle of relations includes all dialects or all living beings within the ecosystem." In this way, the smudged circle is all inclusive and provides a relational framework within how to best work together with the understanding that we are all relatives. Reg further explained the development of this relational framework:

> A group of people coming together to achieve goals and membership is called *kohoihka'si*, a Blackfoot word for an all-friends group. We become relatives, let's say, within the environment, when we need to do something to survive—when we need to come together as a group. We adopt oral terms of reference through making relatives to protect our goals, objectives, and membership—parallel to a legal entity in Western frameworks or organizations. As soon as you come together as a group to achieve whatever you need to achieve or survive together, then you become relatives. And after you become relatives, everything else is your relative. The snow, the rain, the grass are all your relatives. The four seasons become part of your relatives.

The importance of "making relatives" was quickly apparent in the process of developing an Indigenous Strategy for the University of Calgary. To approach the process with the conscious goal of making relatives meant that the institution would acknowledge Indigenous ways of being, knowing, and doing and the cultural and governance protocols embedded within Indigenous communities. That is, the process of developing the strategy had to begin with a commitment to creating two parallel pathways. One would adhere to university committee structures, policy frameworks, and approval procedures; the other would adhere to appropriate cultural protocols, ceremonies, and approval procedures. The creation of these parallel, equal pathways was necessary to come into the circle and relate to one another and our collective work in a meaningful way.

The process of making relatives, or creating and maintaining good relations, was also important in establishing the relational understanding and commitment expected of a traditional, Western, postsecondary institution. In the dominant culture, postsecondary institutions wield tremendous power in the community. Universities are large organizations with long histories and entrenched ways of doing things. They also bring tremendous expertise, respect, and power to relationships. These facts commonly create competition and power imbalances in relationships with postsecondary institutions. In this case, the power dynamics had to change, and the university needed to find ways to rebalance and begin to decolonize those dynamics. The concept of making relatives was a critical foundation for that process. It also served as a constant reminder that humility needed to be invited into the circle in an authentic way.

THE CIRCLE AS A RELATIONAL FRAMEWORK

Most large Western organizations function with an extensive hierarchy and distinctly tiered decision-making protocols. Postsecondary institutions are clear examples of such organizations, and their processes to develop institutional strategies follow hierarchical pathways. In developing an Indigenous Strategy for the University of Calgary, however, these processes needed to make room for frameworks that would reset relationships, or begin new relationships, with Indigenous communities.

This need to create room for a relational framework was articulated by a Traditional Knowledge Keeper during one of our dialogues. He pointed out that Eurocentric decision-making systems are based on positions or levels of authority in an organization. Even within a single committee or decision-making body, these rules apply. Moreover, decisions are made in square rooms and around rectangular tables, meaning that there are implied hierarchies and boundaries even in the physical layouts of spaces.

The parallel framework for development of the strategy had to balance Eurocentric and Indigenous ways of being, knowing, and doing. The Traditional Knowledge Keeper suggested that we needed to understand the power of circles and alternative ways that circles shape decision making. He said that circles place people in positions of equality and require true understanding of others' perspectives. They also encourage collaborative discussions that support non-hierarchical processes that result in stronger relationships among those involved in decision making. We realized that this was both a key dynamic in creating a successful strategy in the short term and a critical aspect of resetting relationships with Indigenous communities in the coming decades. With the importance of the circle as a relational framework, Reg Crowshoe describes the collective intention and relationship created with this critical Indigenous structure and process:

> When I acknowledge all of creation as my relatives, then in natural law nothing in creation is stronger than anybody or anything else. We are all equal. So, in that context, I include everything or all my relatives in my processes and/or practices. So we engage in a practice of sanctified kindness: kindness to all. When you include the environment that you live in, and all creation in that environment, then they all become my relatives in working together to survive. So everybody becomes our relatives.
>
> When you think of relatives, most people look at their own blood relatives or human beings. But in a circle framework, with sanctified kindness and the smudge and the four stories, that relational system of working together to achieve the goal of survival includes all of creation as your relatives. So, when you are part of a group, like the Little Birds, for example, we all become Little Birds, but we also have become relatives. And the Little Birds who were together in a nest last year, they're in a different nest today. Once they leave the Little Birds, they become parents to the new members, and we become little brothers and sisters in the nest, and the Little Birds before them become our grandparents. These "relatives" become our terms of reference and provide and protect our practices.

Coming into the circle therefore represents more than simply making decisions using a process that differs from Western committee procedures and use of the gavel. Instead, it reflects a strong commitment to acknowledge and respect relationships with one another, all creatures and creation, and the lands to which we are connected. Coming into the circle also reflects a commitment to sustain these relationships in a good way. Once entered, they and our obligations to each other continue to exist. This was an integral part of the strategy process since those from the university had to commit to the broad, enduring, covenantal nature of the relationships that we were building. Finally, as Crowshoe suggests, coming into the circle meant that all involved would bring their gifts to the strategy process and both share and mentor where they could. In this way, coming into the circle established a foundation and expectations far different from those that the University of Calgary had ever experienced when developing other institutional strategies.

As emphasized throughout the chapters, establishing parallel pathways that equally represented two unique worldviews, two knowledge systems, and two ways of working together became the hallmark of our process. The normal university process of developing institutional strategies is based on Eurocentric governance structures and written practices. Developing the Indigenous Strategy incorporated typical university processes accompanied and enriched by Indigenous ways of doing through the adoption of a journey framework grounded by ceremonial and oral practices. By coming into the circle, the university fully committed to processes based on oral systems. Indigenous ways of knowing and culturally appropriate ceremonies were vital in this process. Therefore, Traditional Knowledge Keepers became important guides for and connectors of the two worldviews, and they routinely searched for parallels as the process of creating the strategy evolved. Crowshoe summarizes the importance of this search:

> Sometimes the concepts embedded in the language systems don't understand each other. So I can talk to any of our circles in any of our societies about allies and partners. In our language, they understand the idea of achieving goals together; they know what that is, but the concept of allies and partners in the context of Western organizations might not translate, conceptually, to the same understanding. There are different knowledge systems embedded in the languages that we may need to culturally interpret and/or translate so that we can achieve common goals and work together. Cultural interpretation creates space for our oral system. In the written system, the process for achieving goals by bringing people together as a group and creating allies and partners is parallel to making relatives in an oral system. These processes do the same thing. But, in our case, in a different language system, the act of making relatives includes all things in creation. That is an

important part of that relational process, where sanctified kindness is a necessary act of survival within an interconnected ecosystem.

In this way, the University of Calgary's process for developing *ii' taa'poh'to'p* was a complete reimagining of relationships both within postsecondary institutions and with Indigenous communities. The process involved a journey of co-creation with community guided by Indigenous knowledge Keepers. Those involved quickly committed to our parallel journey and were open to listening to, learning from, and taking spiritual guidance from Traditional Knowledge Keepers.

Committing to the Circle

The University of Calgary's Indigenous Strategy represents a commitment to transformation and renewal, looking several generations into the future. It recognizes the need for real and meaningful reconciliation with Indigenous communities and a commitment to become relatives. As such, it is a visionary strategy that will take many years to fulfill in terms of reconciliation between the University of Calgary and Indigenous peoples. *ii' taa'poh'to'p* is a cyclical strategy that engages constant learning, exploration, and evolution.

As a first step, the university dedicated itself to coming into the circle, meaning that it would strive to understand and value Indigenous worldviews as equal to the dominant systems upon which postsecondary institutions have been built. Working with Traditional Knowledge Keepers, the university's Steering Committee and Working Group sought to develop a common understanding and purpose in the process of creating the strategy. The commitment to parallel paths meant that the work was inherently grounded in ceremony and Indigenous ways of knowing and doing. Our journey was informed and shaped by key cultural teachings such as sanctified kindness, parallel paths, and ethical space. It was also an iterative development compelling us to return to the circle for reflective dialogue and ceremonial validation.

A fundamental aspect of the process was the generous sharing of knowledge by Traditional Knowledge Keepers, giving equal status to oral practices. The vulnerability and honest sharing of their lived experiences also deepened an understanding of the impact of colonization and the devastating legacy of residential schools. Some of these teachings and storied experiences led to an epistemic shift in our ways of approaching the strategy by: engaging in the circle and the smudge; reflecting on the critical meaning and nature of stories; and immersing ourselves in the process of making relatives with humility, respect, courage, honesty, and kindness. These foundations articulated systems parallel to Western practice, guiding those tasked with developing the strategy at every step of the process. The journey was an experience of deep learning and personal and collective transformation for those involved. Transformations were the result of the knowledge shared, the relationships built, and the ceremonies experienced, a gift of renewal.

Transitional Story

RECONCILIATION AND VALUES

Reconciliation is a new concept for Canadian society, one with which we have little experience. This is a challenge, for it is difficult to speak about something for which there is little experience. The Truth and Reconciliation Commission has provided a picture of what reconciliation entails with a road map for how we can start on the journey. Reconciliation is increasingly becoming the broad conceptual framework driving Indigenous-related public policy in Canada. It has the power to touch and transform all aspects of Canadian society. As part of the Indigenous Strategy, it is imperative that we take a deep dive into the TRC's materials and develop a strategic response to the 94 Calls to Action and what they mean for the University of Calgary. We must draw from these materials to develop a lexicon for reconciliation and embed this language ubiquitously in the strategy and across campus.

Values are at the heart of the Indigenous Strategy and indigenization more generally. Other factors, such as meaningful engagement of communities, participation of Indigenous peoples in decision making, pedagogies like land-based learning, and the role of Elders and Traditional Knowledge Keepers in course delivery are integral. Yet all these are connected with and informed by values. Grounded in traditional teachings, such ethical values form the basis for decision making and action. For example, understanding the Earth as alive, with all various aspects coming from the Creator, instills values of relationship and respect with an ethics of stewardship. One Elder shared that "You can only take from the land what you need; if you take more, you have to share it." These ethical values inspire principles of sharing and kindness rooted in a profound sense of relationship with a responsibility to care for those relationships.

Shared by the Late Dr. David Lertzman in
Reflective Notes Addressed to Co-Chairs

Our Four-Stage Journey

Reg Crowshoe, Shawna Cunningham, Jacqueline Ottmann, Jackie Sieppert

Four Stories

A PLACE OF CONFLUENCE

I think that Fort Calgary (now called The Confluence) as a venue for the Inner-City Dialogue was so important. There was conversation about what Fort Calgary meant and the actual location of Fort Calgary at the confluence of the Bow and Elbow Rivers and the crossroads of Indigenous and non-Indigenous cultures during the height of colonization—a site traditionally known as Moh'kinstsis to the Blackfoot, Wîchîspa to the Stoney Nakoda, and Guts'ists'i to the Tsuut'ina. Knowing that before we went into that Inner-City Dialogue, triggered conversations about marginalization. We went into community wanting to truly listen to the stories of the people to envision how we, as a large research-intensive university, can become a better relative. We wanted to learn how the university can be of service to community. We wanted to re-imagine how to work with Indigenous and non-Indigenous agencies in a better way, including organizations who are trying to address the marginalization of Indigenous peoples whether in education, employment, or social services. I think both the location and topics covered during that first community dialogue were important touchstones for the journey ahead.

Shawna Cunningham

DEEP RESPONSIBILITY

I can remember just being so exhausted after our Full-Circle Dialogue but also thinking about how much I had learned. How it was unfair that people didn't feel included on our campus or that they were experiencing overt racism. That wasn't right, and it just affirmed, for me, that we had to get the strategy right, and we needed to take our time to do it properly. I also remember meeting with former Assembly of First Nations Grand Chief Perry Bellegarde at the beginning of our journey, and he said to me "It's really great you're doing this, Dru, but don't screw it up." I mean that's how blunt he was. It was not just an obligation to develop this strategy. We felt a deep responsibility that we had to approach this strategy very differently and that we had to do our best to get it right.

Dru Marshall

AMBIGUITY

When the Working Group started its process, we first looked to our other institutional strategies, thinking that there might be ideas or processes there that we could emulate. We realized quickly that our journey would have to be different. I think that the creation of the Indigenous Strategy took much longer than we anticipated and even longer for us to fully process and really understand what the journey meant. We had no idea how different this strategy would be, nor did we have any idea how often our ideas, our process, would shift as we moved through the entire journey. I think that we had the sense that somehow we'd put a plan together, and it would move ahead. But as we worked on the strategy, it seemed to shift every few weeks or every month or two as we learned and our thinking changed. So, if there's one word that I would use to describe those early stages, it is ambiguity. When we began, we weren't sure exactly what the process would look like, but we knew that it was going to be different, and we had to just accept that and go with it.

Jackie Sieppert

SPIRAL APPROACH

"Jagged Worlds Colliding" by Leroy Little Bear (2000) speaks to the impact of colonization on Indigenous worldviews and the resulting and ongoing intercultural tensions. We felt those jagged edges between worldviews throughout the creation of the university's Indigenous Strategy, and we felt the dynamic forces of change within the ethical space that we stepped into—uncertainty, chaos, creativity, adaptation, and innovation. In awakening the spirit of ii' taa'poh'to'p, *we were swept into the challenge of shapeshifting an institution by engaging non-linear processes familiar to Indigenous peoples. The journey was spiral in nature—circles upon circles. We had to address and if possible reconcile the tension caused by old and new learning, identify competing values and faulty belief systems, repeatedly loop back to impactful concepts and stories (Elders'/kēhtē-ayak/chi-anishinaabek ways of transferring knowledge and known as organizational learning), and accept that we would be leaving some things behind so that we could begin the journey on the hazy and windy road ahead of us. I knew that the Indigenous Strategy process had been anticipated by the Indigenous community for some time, and I soon learned that it was something bigger than all of us. It wouldn't have been successful if we didn't continually strive to be in good relations. The sense of responsibility was significant.*

Jacqueline Ottmann

Introduction

The journey to create an Indigenous Strategy began, as most strategies do within postsecondary institutions, with the development of terms of reference, key committees and their members, and expected goals and timelines (University of Calgary 2017b, 40). In the Indigenous Strategy process, however, inclusivity and representation of both Indigenous and non-Indigenous people and worldviews were critical. Efforts were made to include our entire campus community in the process while ensuring the presence of Indigenous voices, which were included at all stages and all levels of our developmental journey. The Indigenous Strategy Task Force included Traditional Knowledge Keepers appointed to the Steering Committee. Indigenous representatives from both the campus and local community organizations were included in the Working Group. Additionally, several ceremonial Elders served as spiritual leaders and cultural advisers throughout the various stages of our journey. With advice and guidance from Traditional Knowledge Keepers, the university created space for a culturally parallel developmental journey:

> The adoption of an Indigenous framework, based upon oral traditions, both acknowledged and honoured cultural parallels between Euro-centric and Indigenous ways of knowing. It also provided an ethically grounded space for community engagement and cultural validation throughout our journey. Each stage of development was validated through ceremony (University of Calgary 2017b, 41).

The development of the University of Calgary Indigenous Strategy was informed, shaped, and enriched by a parallel Indigenous framework. Ceremony became a vital and reflective part of the process, marking important milestones in our journey. Ceremony, within the four-stage journey framework (University of Calgary 2017b, 41), created a safe and ethical space for difficult conversations, engaging members of the Indigenous Task Force in a culturally immersive journey while allowing time for meaningful community engagement.

Our Four-Stage Journey Framework

Early in the development of the university's Indigenous Strategy, Traditional Knowledge Keepers on the Steering Committee advised the provost (Dru Marshall) to begin the process "in a good way" by adopting a parallel framework grounded by Indigenous ways of knowing and doing. The Indigenous co-chairs, Jacqueline Ottmann and Shawna Cunningham, were then tasked to meet with Elder Reg Crowshoe to develop an Indigenous framework to help inform and guide the development of our Indigenous Strategy. The four-stage journey framework adopted for the Indigenous Strategy was based on a previous University of Calgary student-led project called the Cenovus Spo'pi Solar House.[1] This solar-powered home—designed by students in consultation with Elder Reg Crowshoe and the Treaty 7 region—was an entry in the 2011 Solar Decathlon competition held in Washington, DC. The development and design of the Spo'pi house evoked the symbolic representation of a warrior empowered by ceremony at various stages of its journey to Washington and back. Conversations with Elder Crowshoe similarly led to the creation of a four-stage journey framework for the Indigenous Strategy based on historical communal practices associated with land journeys that can involve hunting or gathering food to ensure community sustainability. The framework for the strategy followed the symbolic representation of a group of relatives embarking on a journey to seek, bring home, and partake in sustenance for the community—a journey empowered by ceremony.

STAGE 1: CALLING TOGETHER AND SETTING OUT/ DEVELOPING TERMS OF REFERENCE

The first stage of our ceremonial journey framework was aptly titled Calling Together and Setting Out. The institutional way of doing commenced with the appointment of the Indigenous Task Force, including co-chairs and members of a smaller Steering Committee and a larger Working Group. The co-chairs included pairing an institutional leader with an Indigenous leader from within the university. Dru Marshall, the provost, and Jacqueline Ottmann, a professor in education who had led

---

1   For more information on the Cenovus Spo'pi Solar House, see https://www.solardecathlon.gov/past/2011/where_is_canada_now.

the development of the Indigenous Strategy in the Werklund School of Education, co-chaired the Steering Committee; Jackie Sieppert, dean of the Faculty of Social Work, and Shawna Cunningham, director of the Native Centre (now Writing Symbols Lodge), the Indigenous Student Centre, co-chaired the Working Group. The Steering Committee began to form in the fall of 2015 with traditional institutional terms of reference for the committees being developed. It quickly became apparent that these terms of reference were not going to serve the development of an institutional Indigenous Strategy.

Creation of the parallel Indigenous four-stage journey framework was envisioned after significant conversation with and guidance from Elders. Once that framework came into being, all members of the Indigenous Task Force engaged in a progressive journey of cultural immersion shaped by a regional Indigenous way of doing grounded by ceremony to protect, inform, and celebrate progress:

> the ceremonial initiation of the Steering Committee was marked by a pipe ceremony, held on April 6, 2016. This was followed by the initiation of the Working Group, marked by a smudge ceremony, held on May 18, 2016. All members of the Indigenous Strategy Task Force (members of the Steering Committee and Working Group) were gifted with small Pendleton pouches, symbols of commitment to the development of the strategy. (University of Calgary 2017b, 41)

The pipe ceremony marked a coming together of the Steering Committee in which the co-chairs asked the Elders for ceremonial blessings and ongoing cultural guidance as we embarked on our parallel journey. During this initial ceremony, led by Kainai ceremonial and spiritual leader the late Andy Black Water, the institutional and Indigenous frameworks were treated as parallel documents, blessed and placed alongside one another into a pipe bag kept in the provost's office throughout the journey, awaiting completion of the strategy.

At this stage of our journey, members of the Working Group were gifted with small Pendleton pouches containing sage, sweetgrass, tobacco, cedar, and a small rock. These medicine pouches were gifted in a smudge ceremony led by Elder Reg Crowshoe and blessed multiple times as the group moved from one stage of the journey to the next and/or sought guidance at moments of uncertainty or challenge. Reg became the ceremonial Elder for the Working Group and referred to the medicine pouches as parallel to "membership cards." As our journey progressed, the medicine pouches took on progressive and profound meanings for the individual members of the Working Group and were brought to meetings not just as tokens but also as animated witnesses to the journey, taking on the reflective and transformational energy of lived experiences.

For members of the Indigenous Task Force, this first stage of our journey together in ceremony was a critical part of initiating the development of an Indigenous Strategy for the University of Calgary in a good and parallel way.

STAGE 2: CLEARING THE PATH AND GATHERING STORIES

The second stage of our four-stage journey, Clearing the Path and Gathering Stories, was parallel to Western processes for information gathering through literature reviews, internal and external scans, and narrative data collection, employing methods such as focus groups and community consultations. Since this stage of the journey was comprehensive and formative, we have chosen to share it in two distinct segments.

Clearing the Path

An essential starting point on the journey toward an Indigenous Strategy was to better understand the internal and external contexts for this work. Doing so required background research focused on "three key areas": (1) "developing a sense of readiness" in regard to indigenization, (2) "learning more about what other post-secondary institutions had done with regards to the development of similar strategies," and (3) "understanding the foundational documents that provide the context and history of Indigenous education" (University of Calgary 2017b, 40). As part of the Clearing the Path stage, the Working Group launched and completed three research-based activities to help provide clarity and shape the strategy:

1. a literature review focused on the history and background of Indigenous education in Canada; barriers to education

for Indigenous students; and relevant policies and frameworks to support Indigenous education;

2. an internal environmental scan to identify current strengths and potential gaps in Indigenous education at the University of Calgary; and

3. an external scan and benchmark study to examine other postsecondary institutions across Canada. (University of Calgary 2017b, 41)

Led by key members of the Working Group, the internal scan included a comprehensive survey to be completed by faculties and business units providing information on Indigenous academic and non-academic programs and special initiatives. Information gathered from internal consultations and scans was then compared with information gathered from an external comprehensive literature review identifying and highlighting decolonization theory and practice in postsecondary education. These processes allowed us to better understand where we were as an institution with respect to decolonization and/or indigenization of the academy and to capture wise, innovative practices that might help to inform our journey toward truth and reconciliation.

Consultation included information from an internal scan of our current programs, inclusive practices and policies, and existing community partnerships in academic and research programs. This information helped us to better understand the scope and depth of our current teaching, learning, and research environments. Pockets of excellence within the university, along with areas where significant gaps existed, were also identified. Key members of the Working Group oversaw the collection and organization of information from internal focus groups. These groups covered various sectors of the university community, with participants representing students, student support services, teaching and learning personnel, Indigenous faculty, and deans.

Gathering Stories

Gathering Stories was a fundamental part of the journey toward the development of an Indigenous Strategy for the University of Calgary, informing the content, shaping conceptualizations, and identifying

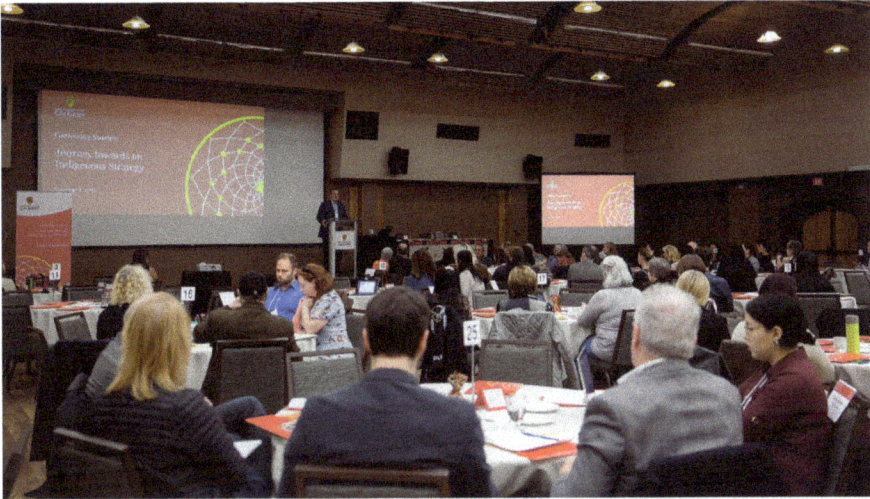

Community Stakeholder (Full Circle) Dialogue. November 4, 2016. University of Calgary. Photo Credit: Riley Brandt, UCalgary.

recommendations. The narrative data collection was grounded in a regional Indigenous paradigm that determined our Indigenous research methodology (Kovach 2009), aligning with the premise that "research is ceremony" (Wilson 2008). Our in-person methods for gathering stories through table conversations and circle dialogues were protected in ceremony and guided by a set of open-ended questions that inspired truth telling (Little Bear 2000; Maracle 2007; Smith 2023), evoking rich narratives based on people's storied experiences. In line with Indigenous ways of knowing and doing, ceremonial blessings became an essential part of opening, closing, and supporting participants during our Gathering Stories community engagement activities. Overall, the Indigenous Strategy Task Force, guided by Traditional Knowledge Keepers, committed to a parallel framework outlining a critical series of internal and external dialogues. A broad process of consultation was designed to be as inclusive as possible and respectful of the Indigenous community, campus community, and other key community stakeholders in both the public and the private sectors. This process was essential in guiding the development of an Indigenous Strategy unique to the University of Calgary.

Cloth bundle of river rocks from Moh'kinstsis. Community Stakeholder (Full Circle) Dialogue. November 4, 2016. University of Calgary. Photo Credit: Riley Brandt, UCalgary.

Our approach was to fully engage the community by embarking on a full-circle reflective journey to gather and listen to stories about indigenizing postsecondary education and the University of Calgary. In addition to the on-campus focus groups, the university hosted three in-person community dialogues: an Inner-City Dialogue, a large Community Stakeholder Dialogue, and a Traditional Knowledge Keepers Dialogue. We also launched an online survey accessible to the university community and the general public. Conversational questions focused on broad topics categorized under the headings "People," "Places," "Programs," and "Practices." Community consultations took place throughout the fall 2016. In total, the university connected with and received input from more than 2,200 people.

The framing of dialogues and the thematic questions on these topics were grounded in the *Final Report of the Truth and Reconciliation Commission of Canada* (TRC 2015) and the compelling call for reconciliation through education, with mindful preparation and consideration for sharing information through an "ethical space of engagement" (Ermine 2007). To create a culturally safe space for sharing stories, the venues for the community dialogues were smudged by an Elder in advance of the gatherings. Once people were gathered, Elders were invited to offer a traditional prayer and ceremonial smudge to open and close each community dialogue in a good way. Cultural hallmarks became important parts of the conversational space, creating a way for participants to listen, pause, reflect, and support one another during the table conversations. These items included beading materials for bracelets and small rocks gathered in a good and reciprocal way from the banks of the Bow River or Moh'kinstsis.

As guests arrived at our storytelling spaces, the tables were adorned with the river rocks wrapped in cloth bundles. The rocks had been cleansed, smudged, and blessed by Elders before being wrapped and placed at the centre of each table. After the opening prayer, individuals were invited to open the cloth bundles to select and hold a rock while listening to and sharing stories. The rocks carried the energy of the individuals who participated in the table conversations, sharing their own stories and listening to those of others. The following explanation, mentioned at the beginning of each community dialogue, was also included on a place card at the centre of each table:

> The rocks situated in the centre of the table come from the Bow River. We ask that you choose a rock for the day and hold on to that rock during our table conversations. The rocks are our grandfathers and will capture the energy of our stories. They connect us to the land and this place we call Moh'kinstsis. At the end of our event, we ask you to take your rock home with you, offer it back to the earth or to the banks of the Bow River, or place it in the cedar basket at the reception table, and we will carefully place it on the grounds of the university as an act of reciprocity.

Beading supplies were also provided at each table, offering an opportunity for individuals to quietly bead colourful bracelets while listening. At the end of the day, many of the individuals offered their bracelets as gifts to others at their table in honour of the stories shared. The exchange of bracelets between individuals, both listeners and storytellers, was relational and heartfelt, serving as a meaningful act of gratitude and reciprocity.

Additionally, we acquired a Pendleton blanket to be used as a ceremonial blanket. This special edition blanket was titled the *Way of Life,*

Bracelet Beading. Community Stakeholder (Full Circle) Dialogue. November 4, 2016. University of Calgary. Photo Credit: Riley Brandt, UCalgary.

which resonated with our journey and parallel paths. The blanket accompanied us to each event and became a witness to our in-person dialogues and ceremonial milestones. It accrued meaning. It was placed on podiums, reception tables, and the head table for the Full-Circle Dialogue. Since the launch of the strategy, this blanket has become our ceremonial blanket, reminding us of our transformational journey—where we were, where we are, and where we are going. It serves as a reminder of our past and our present commitment to the journey of *ii' taa'poh'to'p.*

The dialogues that took place during our table conversations required us to create a culturally safe space for sharing stories and lived experiences. To gain insight into the current and historical relationship between community members and the university, we made a conscious decision to take the role of listener rather than presenter throughout our community consultations. What we heard from our respective community members was invaluable in informing the strategy and envisioning our path forward. To create a culturally safe, ethical space for dialogue, a ceremonial Elder arrived early to each location to cleanse the venue with a smudge.

Additionally, to ground the conversation and open our events in a good way, an Elder offered an opening prayer and a ceremonial smudge at the beginning of each gathering.

Conversations covered a breadth of topics including but not limited to the inclusion of Indigenous knowledge systems and Knowledge Keepers in research, teaching, and learning; the need for meaningful representation of Indigenous peoples in academia (students, staff, and faculty); systemic barriers and challenges associated with postsecondary education in general and the University of Calgary in particular; explorations of new ideas and opportunities for community-informed programs and research partnerships; and the lack of societal and institutional (student, staff, and faculty) knowledge of Indigenous peoples' histories, cultures, diversity, and lived experiences. Each day was closed in a good way, with reflective remarks and a closing prayer.

Community Dialogues

We determined that it was critical to engage in comprehensive consultations with the Indigenous and non-Indigenous communities on and off campus. We embarked on this journey with no preconceived ideas of what our strategy might look like. The ambiguity created space for creativity and voices to be heard during table conversations. Our intent was to listen in order to respond appropriately to the call to create more respectful and meaningful inclusion of Indigenous peoples and Indigenous knowledge systems in postsecondary education. Going to the community before drafting an Indigenous Strategy felt like the right thing to do. Our approach was to ensure that our strategy was not only about the university but also about Indigenous histories, education (including residential school experiences), the impact of colonization, societal and systemic Indigenous racism, as well as shared hope for a better future.

For the larger gatherings, members of the Working Group facilitated table conversations, students were recruited to take notes, and Indigenous scholars and community members were appointed as reflective listeners, moving from one table to another to capture highlights and report back at the end of the day. To better understand the significance of our conversations with the community, which formed the basis of our Indigenous Strategy, we provide a summary of community consultations and dialogues below.

The Inner-City Dialogue

The Inner-City Dialogue, held at Fort Calgary on October 17, 2016, was the first of three important circle dialogues hosted by the university as part of our Gathering Stories phase of development. Fort Calgary is an important place both culturally and historically, a natural place to begin the Indigenous Strategy dialogues.

The purpose of this gathering was to connect with inner-city agencies to gain a better understanding of what the university means to the community and how we could be of service in creating a more welcoming, accepting, and inclusive space. We wanted to know how to further the educational aspirations of Indigenous students and close the gap in the marginalization of Indigenous peoples and communities. Below is a high-level summary of the Inner-City Dialogue:

> This community dialogue focused on the university as a service provider to the community and table conversations addressed marginalization, access to education, and community-based research. Approximately 75 people representing 35 agencies, including First Nations, Métis and Inuit representatives from the City of Calgary and surrounding area attended this event. The table conversations provided insight into the educational barriers, the importance of community partnership, and the overall perception of the University of Calgary from an urban orientation. (University of Calgary 2017b, 42)

We thought that it was critical to start with inner-city voices and stories to disrupt the extractive and presumptuous ways in which many of these conversations started in the past.

The following questions were posed during the table conversations.

Table Conversation 1: People

1. What is the first thing you think about when you look back on your school experience?

2. Did you attend postsecondary? Why/why not?

Table Conversation 2: Programs

3. What challenges or barriers do Indigenous learners face when trying to enter higher levels of education?

4. What can the University of Calgary do to alleviate some of these challenges or barriers?

Table Conversation 3: Practices

5. What can the university do to create a more welcome and inclusive campus for Indigenous learners and community members?

6. What kinds of partnerships with community members, agencies, or organizations should the university pursue to enhance inclusivity for Indigenous learners on campus?

Table Conversation 4: Places/Spaces

7. What kinds of educational programs might the university provide to better serve Indigenous students/communities?

8. How can the university be of service to Indigenous agencies and communities when it comes to research?

These open-ended questions served as conversational guides, and individuals shared rich, diverse perspectives and personal experiences throughout the day. Each table included a host and scribe responsible for moderating the conversation and capturing the essence of the topics addressed. The enthusiastic and emotional conversations were inspiring and challenging, providing insights into how education has failed Indigenous peoples and how the university can reposition itself to be of service to the community in the future by becoming more inclusive of, respectful of, and accessible to Indigenous peoples.

The Community Stakeholder (Full-Circle) Dialogue

The Community Stakeholder Dialogue on November 4, 2016, also referred to as our full-circle gathering, included select agencies, community representatives, community leaders, and First Nations colleges, students, faculty, and staff. Below is a summary of the gathering:

> The full-day event included keynote addresses by Dr. Shauneen Pete, Dr. Willie Littlechild, and Kainai Elder Wilton Goodstriker. The event included conversational questions organized into four topics: people, programs, practices, and places. Table conversations were rich, engaging, and informative. Each table included a facilitator and scribe. Findings and summaries of the table conversations were transcribed and included in the *University of Calgary Indigenous Strategy Data Analysis Report* (March 2017) for the full *Gathering Stories* community engagement series. Approximately 225 stakeholders from 59 agencies, including First Nations, Métis, and Inuit representatives from across Alberta, attended this event. (University of Calgary 2017b, 42)

The table conversations were guided by the following questions.

Table Conversation 1: People

1. How can we ensure the University of Calgary is more accessible to and inclusive of Indigenous peoples?

2. How can the University of Calgary become more culturally competent in relation to Indigenous peoples?

Table Conversation 2: Programs

3. How can we respectfully bridge Indigenous knowledge(s) and practices with the University of Calgary's teaching and learning?

4. What kinds of academic programs will create authentic cultural learning opportunities for Indigenous and non-Indigenous students at the University of Calgary?

Table Conversation 3: Practices

5. How can the University of Calgary best serve Indigenous peoples, communities, and organizations through research?

6. How should the University of Calgary engage community stakeholders in measuring the success of an Indigenous Strategy as we move forward?

Table Conversation 4: Places/Spaces

7. What kinds of places and spaces can the University of Calgary create to enhance its connection with Indigenous peoples and identity in the traditional landscape?

We invited Dr. Shauneen Pete (formerly from the University of Regina) and Dr. Willie Littlechild (commissioner, Truth and Reconciliation Commission) to set the tone and provide context for the table conversations. Each speaker provided a distinct tone, context, and meaning to the work of reconciliation: one focused on the importance of reconciliation and the other on truthing.

Pete, who spoke in the morning, shared a powerful vision of Indigenous peoples' thriving economy and education throughout North America prior to colonization through story, and then she called for the audience members to act, to help right wrongs, and to make our future better, all the while focusing on the role of settler-colonial society. Her essential message was that Indigenous peoples have done their work coping with oppression; systemic, covert, and overt racism; and historical and current impacts of colonization. She called on settlers to increase their understanding of Indigenous experiences in Canada and to acknowledge their role in systemic oppression. Her message was straightforward and simple: to achieve reconciliation, settlers should determine individual and collective actions that will enable them to become part of the solution. This was a bold, important, yet uncomfortable message for many, compelling some individuals to walk out of the room and others to take immediate responsibility and action.

Littlechild spoke in the afternoon. He shared his experiences in the residential school system through first-hand accounts accompanied by poignant images of residential school settings and experiences. His story touched the hearts of many listeners and brought to life the tragic experiences of Indigenous children who attended residential schools—those who survived, those who did not, and those whose lives were forever affected and changed by the scars of deep personal and intergenerational trauma. His message emphasized the importance of truthing as the forerunner to reconciliation, compelling us to take immediate and meaningful action to transform the education system. His message amplified the gravity and significance of the work before the Indigenous Task Force.

To summarize the conversation that took place throughout the day, four Indigenous attendees served as reflective listeners, moving from one table to the next. This group came together as a panel to highlight what they heard based on what resonated for each of them. To close the day in a good way, Kainai Elder Wilton Goodstriker offered grounding remarks and a closing prayer. In later reflective conversations, Jacqueline Ottmann noted that:

> It was a powerful day. It was also a demonstration of ethical space. The format was very intentional. We organized the tables in a way in which university representatives like students, faculty, staff, and administrators could sit together with Indigenous community members and community partners to engage in conversations where they were sharing, listening, and truly hearing each other. So it wasn't a table of deans; it wasn't a table of students; it was a coming together of people not roles. Individuals taking part in the table conversations were hearing various perspectives and hopefully valuing those perspectives.

The venue for this gathering, like the others, was carefully prepared through the smudge, the presence of grandfather rocks, the making and gifting of beaded bracelets, and the opening and closing prayers from Traditional Knowledge Keepers. This ceremonial preparation created a culturally safe, protected space for sharing stories. As Reg Crowshoe reminded us throughout the journey, which included our community gatherings, ceremonies, and meetings, "be sure to bring your *true self.*"

The Traditional Knowledge Keepers Dialogue

The intention behind this gathering on November 18, 2016, was to gain insight into and wisdom from respected Traditional Knowledge Keepers in three areas: Indigenous land, language, and Traditional Knowledge. The gathering included fifteen Indigenous Traditional Knowledge Keepers from the Alberta region and the Calgary community. The dialogue was co-chaired by Dru Marshall and Jacqueline Ottmann, and the conversation was moderated by Phil Fontaine. Below is a brief summary of this gathering:

> This very important session was facilitated by former Assembly of First Nations (AFN) National Chief, Dr. Phil Fontaine, and included participation from 15 Traditional Knowledge Keepers, including First Nations and Métis representatives. The session also included 25 witnesses/listeners. The dialogue focused on Indigenous knowledge in relation to land, language, history, and education. The information shared throughout the day was rich and enlightening and will help to envision the role of the university with respect to Traditional Knowledge and Traditional Knowledge Keepers. (University of Calgary 2017b, 42–43)

In response to key questions posed, the Elders shared individual stories, reflections, and lived experience in circular conversational storytelling format.

The conversational guideline for this day included the following topical questions.

Indigenous Land

1. What does the university community need to understand, and learn about, in terms of our (people's) relationship to land from an Indigenous perspective?

Indigenous Language

2. How can the university best support the revitalization of Indigenous languages in teaching and learning?

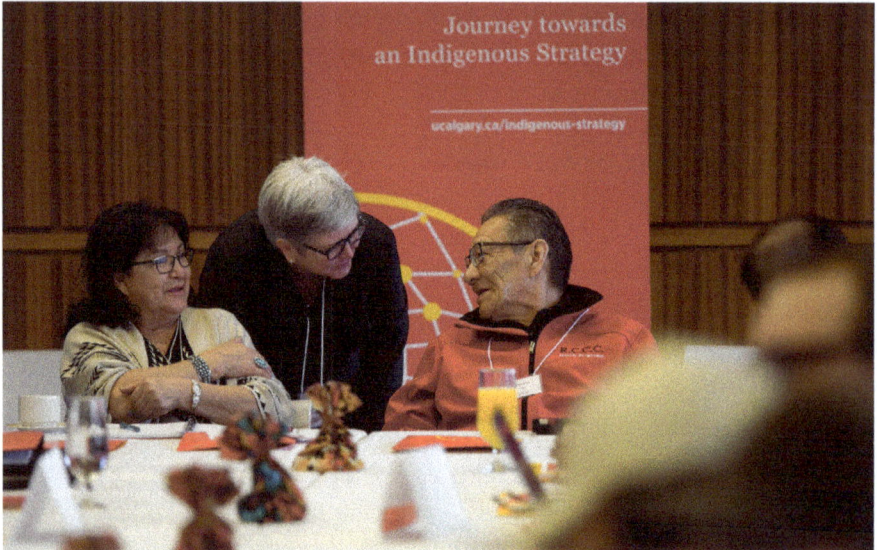

Left to right: Elder Evelyn Goodstiker, Dr. Dru Marshall, Elder Calvin Williams. Traditional Knowledge Keepers Dialogue. November 18, 2016. University of Calgary. Photo Credit: Riley Brandt, UCalgary.

Indigenous Ways of Knowing

3. How can the university best weave Indigenous perspectives and worldviews into the practice of teaching, learning, and research?

Throughout the day, there was fluidity in the storytelling. Although the conversation was guided by questions, the dialogue was not contained by those questions. Through the questions, Elders engaged in an open table conversation sharing their lived experiences, stories, and Traditional Knowledge. The stories shared and the teachings offered were profound, highlighting the violent acts of genocide on Indigenous peoples, languages, and distinct knowledge systems, calling simultaneously for healing and cultural resurgence. We share in more detail in the next chapter a summary of the secular, epistemic, and metaphorical dialogue with Traditional Knowledge Keepers.

The Online Public Survey

To broaden the scope of consultation, the university decided to launch a public survey from November 4 to December 5, 2016. To be consistent, the survey questions mirrored the full-circle table conversations as a congruent data-gathering tool. Because the data gathered did not include in-person dialogue, which can open various conversational trajectories, the survey included an additional catch-all question: "Is there anything that has been missed or ideas you would like to add to this dialogue?"

The survey, open to constituents of the university and members of the public, provided aggregate quantitative data that captured categories of respondents and their relationships with the university, including faculty, staff, students, alumni, and community members. For various reasons, this type of aggregate data was not gathered from participants who attended the in-person gatherings. This additional layer of data was informative when cross-referenced with questions related to intercultural capacity and the desire to support the university and engage in efforts at reconciliation. "Over 1,370 respondents took the time to complete the survey, with the resulting information being comprehensive and informative" (University of Calgary 2017b, 43).

The broad, open-ended questions garnered rich narrative responses and themes that helped us to understand not only our relationships with Indigenous peoples and communities but also the overall knowledge and cultural illiteracy of the campus community with respect to Indigenous peoples, defining the journey ahead and informing the overall content of our strategy. Since the survey was anonymous, we also encountered comments that reflected the deeper layers of overt and systemic racism. Although these comments were not surprising, they were disturbing and yet again compellingly informative about the undercurrents of racism in our society and the challenges that we face as we work toward reconciliation.

To summarize, our Clearing the Path and Gathering Stories stage of development, information gathered from individuals who completed the online survey, was integrated into our narrative data summary report. Information gathered from the literature review, internal and external scans, and in-person and online community consultations was carried into the next stage.

STAGE 3: BRINGING THE STORIES HOME

The third stage of our journey entailed reviewing and considering the information provided by summary reports of internal and external scans, the literature review, and summary reports from the Gathering Stories stage.

With assistance from Indigenous doctoral students and two non-Indigenous faculty members, Jacqueline Ottmann led the narrative analysis of the three in-person community engagement dialogues as well as the raw data gathered from responses to the online public survey. Additionally, other campus leaders and members of the Working Group integrated the results of the university-wide internal scan and an external scan that provided information on how other select postsecondary institutions were responding to the marginalization of Indigenous peoples. A final summary report on the narrative data was compiled and brought to the Steering Committee and Working Group for reflection. Once approved, this report was handed off to a subcommittee of the Working Group. Writing the strategy was a collective endeavour fully based on this summary report, called *What We Heard*.

STAGE 4: EMPOWERING THE SPIRIT OF INDIGENIZATION

Empowering the Spirit of Indigenization was the final stage of our four-stage journey framework. This stage—which included ceremonial validation, transfers, and cultural gifting marking the progress, milestones, and key accomplishments of our journey—ran parallel to university approval processes. Although ceremonial validation was important, there was the practical task of moving the Indigenous Strategy, a somewhat atypical document, through various levels of institutional approval, in line with traditional university processes. Cultural translation therefore played a significant and emergent role in guiding the strategy through the university approval processes and Indigenous ceremonial practices. Cultural interpretation between the university and the Indigenous community was required not only to explain the parallel paths taken to develop the strategy but also to translate and contextualize the Indigenous knowledge embedded in the strategy document itself. Cultural interpretation (cultural brokering, code-talking) was anticipated and realized throughout the development of the Indigenous Strategy but became critical as we moved simultaneously through the university approvals and cultural validation ceremonies necessary to realize empowerment of the strategy.

Championing the strategy through institutional approval and Indigenous validation processes while navigating the two distinct systems (written and oral) required skilled leadership, a mindful approach, and knowledgeable expertise—in other words, the right individuals from the perspectives of both systems. From an institutional perspective, Dru Marshall, our provost at the time, took great care to update the university leadership and the campus community throughout development and at every opportunity, clearly articulating and reiterating our unique and inclusive parallel paths. From an Indigenous knowledge Keeper perspective, Elder Reg Crowshoe continually located and articulated the cultural parallels between the university written system and an Indigenous oral system. He provided ongoing guidance and ceremonial leadership about and throughout the four-stage journey. He worked alongside other ceremonial Elders and the Indigenous community to support the strategy and validate progress as we came together in ceremony to address challenges and celebrate milestones in our journey. Together, Marshall and Crowshoe took on emergent but significant roles as key cultural translators in support of the development, approval, and validation of the strategy, constantly and consistently building relationships and increasing understanding, both within and outside the university. These roles, not always easy, helped to garner and maintain much needed support for the strategy from the university campus and the local Indigenous community. In retrospect, our chosen parallel paths required compassionate and skilled cultural interpretation to articulate and navigate two disparate systems in support of the strategy and the work of the Indigenous Steering Committee and Working Group, ultimately Empowering the Spirit of Indigenization through *ii' taa'poh'to'p*.

Validating the Strategy

Breathing life into the strategy was evoked through ceremony, creating a living document to last for generations to come. June 21, 2017, was a significant date for the Indigenous Strategy. This was the day that the university received ceremonial validation for the proposed strategy, marked by traditional gifts and transfers. These processes of validation paralleled institutional approvals. Transfers and gifts bestowed in honour of the strategy included the following.

1. The late Kainai spiritual leader Andy Black Water bestowed a traditional Blackfoot name for the strategy, *ii' taa'poh'to'p* (meaning a place to rejuvenate and re-energize during a journey). This gift was requested in the initial pipe ceremony in 2016.

2. Elder Reg Crowshoe designed and transferred symbols representing a cultural interpretation of the model.

3. Stoney Nakoda Traditional Knowledge Keeper Rod Hunter transferred an honour song to the University of Calgary.

4. A pipe bag was gifted by the Elders to serve as a journey/mandate bundle[2] for the cultural gifts, the strategy documents, and future gifts and documents associated with the strategy.

In line with our parallel paths, the Indigenous Strategy written document was brought forward to the General Faculties Council for approval on October 19, 2017, and the Board of Governors on October 20 as part of institutional approval. The public launch of the strategy was held on November 16. This community celebration included a transfer of the strategy in which the Indigenous and institutional frameworks, the final strategy document called *ii' taa'poh'to'p*, and the cultural symbols were bundled together in a pipe bag and transferred from the Office of the Provost and Vice-President (Academic) to the Office of the President and Vice-Chancellor in a ceremony. Susan Mide Kiss, a member of the Working Group and co-chair of the launch event, offered the following reflection in a written submission in 2024:

---

2   The term "journey/mandate bundle" is distinct from the sacred bundles associated with traditional sacred societies.

Together with Elder Dr. Reg Crowshoe and other university and community leaders, we co-created the strategy and co-led the launch of *ii' taa'poh'to'p*. The launch was critical to the conceptual and cultural framework, empowering the spirit of reconciliation, inclusive of Indigenous ways of knowing, doing, being, and connecting. Like the co-creation of the strategy, the launch was community-led and engaged, reinforcing the power of learning and working together in parallel ways. The realization, launch, and journey of *ii' taa'poh'to'p* would not be possible without the spiritual support and guidance of Elders Reg and Rose Crowshoe and so many other Indigenous, university and community leaders.

As Elder Reg eloquently stated, "it was a good day for *ii' taa'poh'to'p*."

Transitional Story

ENTRUSTED STORIES

Responsibility for hearing stories requires a commitment and mindfulness to do work in a good way, knowing that what we do now, how our story unfolds and is told, is witnessed by those who have gone before us, experienced by people today, and will impact those not yet born, well into the future. Many understand this way of perceiving and living in the world. We embody it. These people, and more, came to our gatherings. They demonstrated their trust by gifting their time and stories, which they shared courageously and honestly. They told their experiences and hearts' desires because, as some people said to me, they hoped that the University of Calgary will use their stories for good. Because of these gatherings and the online survey, we now have witnesses on and off campus, in Calgary, Alberta, Canada, and internationally, watching for what we, the University of Calgary, will do next.

Jacqueline Ottmann

What We Heard

Jacqueline Ottmann, Jackie Sieppert, Shawna Cunningham

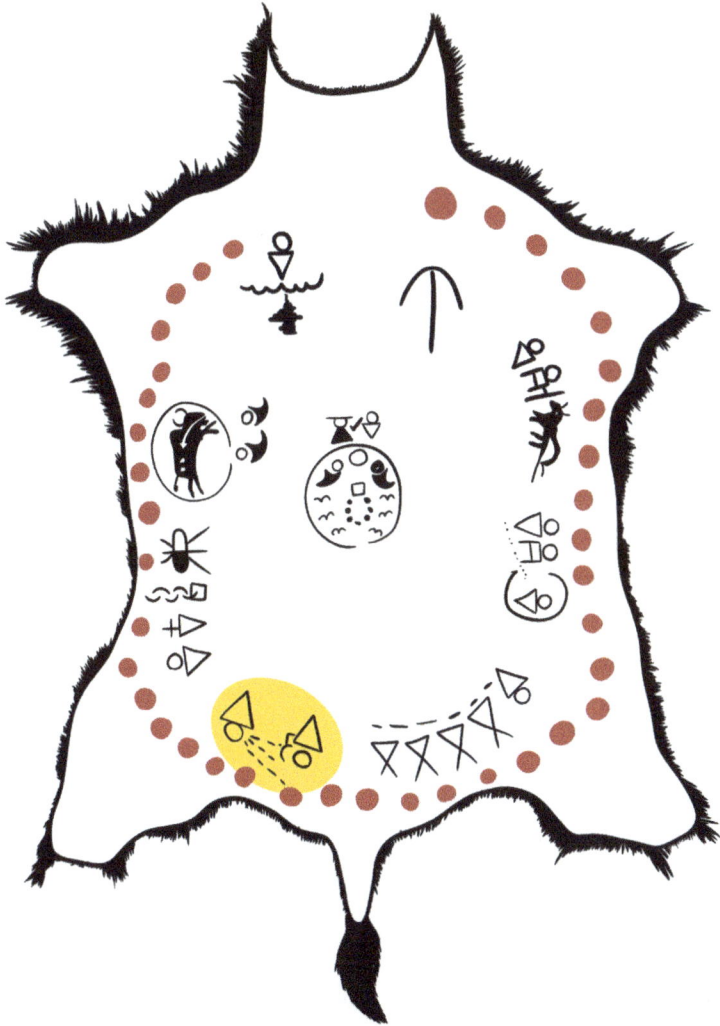

Four Stories

LISTENING

We didn't go to the community with a draft document in hand. We didn't manipulate the process in terms of anticipating where we would land or what the final strategy would look like. We went to the community with an open heart and open mind, and we just listened. And what we heard—all of those words, the stories, and the essence of them—is reflected in our strategy. In looking back, I am grateful for our approach. I felt like we had a humble approach as listeners, and I think we truly did listen. During our community dialogues, we also had others in the room who were reflective listeners. They visited each of the tables throughout the day to capture nuances of conversations as they were unfolding. We had note takers, but we really needed that heart connection—an introspective listener or reflective witness to move from table to table to get a sense of how the dialogue was going and how people were responding to some of the questions that we put to the table.

Shawna Cunningham

HARD STORIES

During the Gathering Stories phase of our process, we learned of the stories of residential school survivors here in our area. I am sure that these stories were hard to tell—I know that they were very difficult to hear. We appreciated the gift of hearing these stories—they strengthened our resolve and sense of responsibility and obligation to make sure that we got the strategy right. We learned of overt racism on our campus—from both students and staff— these stories were also hard to hear, and frankly it is unacceptable that these stories exist on our campus. We must tackle the issue of racism head on if we are truly going to create a campus where everyone feels valued and included.

Dru Marshall

SQUARE CORNERS AND CIRCLES

The other comment that stands out from the Elders' dialogue was a private comment made in passing by one of the Elders. The Elder said to me, "Everything on this campus has square corners, and that's the way that all of you are trained to think." It's a very structured approach to the world. And the Elder said, "We don't think in square corners, we think in circles, and you need to understand what that means." And at first glance it's a simple statement, but as I've thought about it now for a few years, to me it reflects a very different foundational assumption about how the world works and how we all interact with one another and our obligations to one another. So that simple statement about square corners and circles still has me thinking how do I change my assumptions about the world to get rid of square corners?

Jackie Sieppert

COMING TOGETHER

I recall being touched and excited about layering our gatherings with Indigenous ways of doing: creating ethical spaces, talking circles, beading, Pendleton pouches with rocks from Moh'kinstsis, Elders' prayers, pipe ceremonies, the sweet smell of sweetgrass and sage smudge, Indigenous speakers and stories. It seemed surreal. With these traditional practices, I hoped that the Indigenous people who attended the dialogue sessions would feel affirmed and summon the courage to share truths and be honest about their overall relationship with schooling. I also hoped that non-Indigenous participants would appreciate the symbolism and the different ways of coming together. I witnessed people truly listen to each other and some otherwise soft-spoken individuals exercise their voices. As a community, we were envisioning a new future. As I walked around the room of the largest intercultural gathering that we hosted, I felt the energy in the room: apprehension, fear, nervousness, excitement, appreciation, hope, and happiness.

Jacqueline Ottmann

Bringing the Stories Home

The third stage of our Indigenous journey framework entailed the review and analysis of large amounts of information compiled from diverse sources. This began with campus leaders and members of the Working Group who compiled information from the university-wide internal scan, a series of campus focus groups, and an external scan that provided information on where other postsecondary institutions were at in terms of Indigenous programming, strategic development, and responses to the *Final Report of the Truth and Reconciliation Commission of Canada* (TRC 2015). To this foundation, we then added narrative data from our in-person community dialogues. Notetakers captured the narratives, which included many vital stories shared by individuals who participated in the dialogues and table conversations. Finally, we compiled and integrated the results from on-campus focus groups and the online survey into these analyses. For the survey, we analyzed responses to open-ended questions and added the results to the data that guided development of the Indigenous Strategy.

Key leaders guided the analysis. With assistance from gifted doctoral students Vicki Bouvier (Métis/Michif) and Gabrielle Lindstrom (Kainai/Blackfoot), and two faculty members, David Lertzman and Jim Frideres, Jacqueline Ottmann (Anishinaabe) led the narrative analysis of the three in-person community engagement dialogues: the Inner-City Dialogue, the Stakeholders/Full-Circle Dialogue, and the Traditional Knowledge Keepers Dialogue. The narrative data/stories went through a rigorous coding process done manually and through NVivo.[1] Ottmann, Bouvier, and Lindstrom, the data analysis team, came together each week to discuss the process and progress of the analysis (e.g., words and phrases that formed the codes [nodes] and emerging findings, discussion of quotations that supported the findings). The team then analyzed textual data from the 1,370 respondents who completed an online survey available to the internal and external communities from November 4 to December 5, 2016.

The extensive narrative findings from the community dialogues and public survey were integrated into a summary report. The results presented here were drawn from that report. The findings from these diverse

---

1   NVivo is a qualitative analysis software program by Lumivero; see https://lumivero.com/.

and rich sources of data represent "what we heard" to guide the journey toward an Indigenous Strategy.

Rather than detailing specific results from each data source, in this chapter we "bring the stories home" by organizing information into five core themes identified from the analyses: (1) understanding barriers to postsecondary education, (2) challenging institutional myths about Indigenous peoples, (3) becoming a welcoming place, (4) expanding worldviews, and (5) listening deeply to Traditional Knowledge Keepers. We begin by reflecting on potential barriers that Indigenous students face when considering postsecondary education.

UNDERSTANDING BARRIERS TO POSTSECONDARY EDUCATION

Important stories about the significant barriers that Indigenous students face emerged from the first moments of our consultations—the Inner-City Dialogue held at Fort Calgary. At that event, we hoped to hear stories that would help us to understand how the University of Calgary was perceived in our community. It was also important to learn more about how community members imagined ways that the university could be of service through teaching, learning, research, and partnerships. What we heard most powerfully, though, were descriptions of negative experiences with school systems and several deeply personal stories about why Indigenous people did not attend postsecondary institutions.

For many, the first thing that came to mind when thinking about postsecondary education was the challenge of coming from families or communities where education was valued but not accessible because of societal, economic, academic barriers, and the lack of family support given negative perceptions of Eurocentric education systems. This was not a surprise to us. Education was described as a struggle and difficult to access for reasons related to historical efforts at assimilation (e.g., systemic barriers legislated by the Indian Act, Indian residential schools, permit systems, enfranchisement). It was clear that the residential school experience and the associated trauma of physical, verbal, and emotional violence are still present and continue to profoundly shape experiences of education.

Participants pointed to several core challenges stemming from their negative experiences with Western systems, such as low achievement results, the lack of diversity on university campuses, struggles with addiction, trauma, and funding shortfalls. Being the first family member to attend a postsecondary institution was also described as difficult because of culture shock, unfamiliarity with the processes, expectations, and ways of navigating funding and program scheduling.

Prior experiences with dominant school systems have been problematic for many Indigenous people. For many who responded to us, schooling meant struggles, alienation, isolation, and a general lack of support. Some participants shared their residential school experiences and stories of being forced to go to school. Moreover, some thought that they were never a part of the school environment because generally there was a small number of Indigenous students in rural and urban schools. This was compounded by the absence of Indigenous cultural presence in our education systems. For some, not seeing references to their own cultures created the feeling of isolation and a sense that postsecondary institutions generally were unwelcoming to Indigenous students. Multiple participants asserted that there is a lack of recognition and understanding of Indigenous students' adverse life experiences, including trauma, loss, poverty, racism, and social marginalization.

Having a strong sense of Indigenous identity was described as important to the process of education, and those struggling with their own identities expressed doubts about postsecondary education. In the dialogues, some participants talked about their experiences of being "mixed-race" and how it challenged the development of a healthy sense of Indigenous identity. Some thought that those in "mainstream society" often conceptualized indigeneity as deficient and that this conception created a significant barrier to their participation in higher education. They indicated that such a perspective negatively affected their self-esteem and resulted in a tenuous relationship with their Indigenous identities. In general, some participants thought that they did not look Indigenous enough, whereas others felt the need to hide their indigeneity.

These questions of identity were clearly related to stories of racism and exclusion. Racism was consistently identified as a concerning and recurring theme in our data collection. In some of the table conversations at our community dialogues, participants mentioned that they had been dealing with racism since childhood. Many also said that racism among students, teachers, and administrators had continued into their postsecondary experiences. We heard stories of professors and other students who had told Indigenous students that they should just take Native Studies courses or that the university's Native Centre was not equipped to deal with racism on campus. Several participants noted that educational institutions, including universities, lack the necessary emotional, mental, and spiritual supports to ameliorate or manage the effects of racism and racial violence for Indigenous students, staff, and faculty. That is, the lack of campus-wide action plans aimed at combatting racism was seen as a significant barrier for Indigenous students at postsecondary institutions.

Importantly, examples of racism went beyond the stories told by Indigenous participants in our consultations. Analysis of comments submitted through the public survey also revealed clear and troubling racism. Although few, these overt comments revealed that racism toward Indigenous people was real on our campus and would have to be overcome if we were to be truly supportive of Indigenous students, staff, and faculty.

Several Indigenous learners pointed, of course, to university structures and processes as substantial barriers to postsecondary education. Many suggested that processes to access postsecondary education were rigid and focused on measures of educational success that reward Eurocentric ways of knowing. Existing university policies were also described as narrowly defined and exclusionary. Examples included postsecondary recruitment procedures, entrance requirements, timelines, and discrepant expectations between reserve and provincial schools.

Another significant barrier identified throughout our conversations was the lack of funding for Indigenous students across Canada. The dialogues included comments from or about individuals who were accepted into programs but were unable to attend them because of the lack of postsecondary funding. Participants also commented about insufficient funding available to individual First Nations students. Some pointed to challenges with sponsorship opportunities available through the Post-Secondary Student Support Program (PSSSP) funded by Indigenous Services Canada. They described the PSSSP as insufficient since the federal program does not cover the number of First Nations students who apply and are eligible for sponsorship. Participants said that PSSSP sponsorship is difficult to receive, and if received the amount allocated to individuals does not meet the increasingly high costs of education and living.

Despite the significant obstacles that Indigenous students face in seeking postsecondary education, our research analysis also identified a strong sense of optimism about the roles of universities in supporting Indigenous people. Despite the challenges associated with postsecondary education, some participants highlighted positive schooling experiences. They believed that education is an opportunity for self-discovery and to learn about Indigenous histories and current issues in Canada, especially regarding residential schools and Indigenous identities. Some participants noted that education is a source of hope for Indigenous people and that school is important. The positive aspects of the educational experience might be conceptualized as a range of protective factors that help mitigate challenges created by colonized school systems. Indigenous people might be more likely to overcome the lack of Indigenous cultural presence on campus if they have a keen sense of personal determination to contribute to their communities.

CHALLENGING MYTHS ABOUT INDIGENOUS PEOPLES

Discussion related to the institution's inclusion of Indigenous peoples and cultural competence revealed several important themes centred on the need to dispel prevalent myths about Indigenous peoples. The first might be framed best by a concept called the "affective domain," which refers to an emotive dynamic that, in this case, maintains and perpetuates negative conceptualizations of Indigenous peoples (Krathwohle, Bloom, and Masia 1973).[2]

Using the affective domain to analyze the emotive aspects of the data, we discovered that participants wanted negative attitudes and affective conceptualizations about Indigenous peoples to change. This was a significant and recurring theme across the dialogue sessions. Negative conceptualizations identified during table conversations included perception of or actual exposure to elitist attitudes among some University of Calgary

---

2   The affective domain includes how we deal with things emotionally, such as feelings, values, appreciation, enthusiasm, motivation, and attitude.

faculty members and leaders. Some Indigenous community members perceived the university itself as intimidating and postsecondary education as unattainable. They noted that challenging and changing attitudes, values, and belief systems of the dominant society will also change how people interact, thereby increasing the long-term quality of relationships.

A subtheme of "epistemic conflicts" (Wagner 2021) also emerged in our sessions. Epistemic conflicts are reflected in or emerge as racism, discrimination, and persistent marginalization of Indigenous peoples. Examples included the "othering" (Ahmed 2002 ; Spivak 1988) of Indigenous knowledge systems, implying that traditional Indigenous knowledge is inferior to Western knowledge—leading to the continued marginalization of Indigenous ways of knowing and doing in the academy. Epistemic conflicts are essentially clashes of worldviews, linked theoretically to *epistemic violence* and the colonization and imminent marginalization of others (Spivak 1988).

Throughout our dialogue sessions, but especially in our on-campus dialogues, there was a strong call to increase awareness of the lived realities of Indigenous peoples among non-Indigenous staff, faculty, and students. This included a demand that non-Indigenous members of the university learn about the histories and current realities of Indigenous peoples and their worldviews/perspectives.

Participants suggested that acknowledging these lived realities is critical to building relationships that help students to succeed. Front-line staff members, especially those working closely with Indigenous students, need opportunities to develop their knowledge, learn about the challenges that Indigenous students face, and realize how negative experiences affect the university experience. New faculty or employee "onboard" training needs to incorporate Indigenous facilitation of authentic content to generate understanding and empathy. Participants also mentioned ongoing professional development as important, with suggestions that non-Indigenous university members should learn about the TRC (2015) Calls to Action.

One element under the topic of "challenging myths regarding Indigenous peoples" did relate specifically to those Calls to Action. We heard demands that the University of Calgary respond to the calls. Many participants suggested that a first step would be to ensure that university staff are knowledgeable about Indigenous students' realities, histories, issues, and barriers. Some suggested that this training be mandatory for all university personnel. They described this kind of professional learning as one way to increase the overall cultural competencies among non-Indigenous people.

Finally, data from the survey identified a general need to change the negative attitudes toward Indigenous peoples and cultures. A deeply entrenched colonial history has influenced the belief systems of Canadian society (often resulting in micro-aggression and biased behaviour), and colonial mindsets, behaviours, and policies are evident in education systems. Some participants suggested that anti-racist, anti-oppressive pedagogies be included in faculty and staff professional development programs to combat racist and discriminatory attitudes and actions and false information about Indigenous peoples. We were disappointed to see clearly, if not prevalent, racist comments from a small number of survey respondents.

Becoming More Welcoming

At the first Inner-City Dialogue held at Fort Calgary, several participants mentioned that postsecondary institutions are isolating and marginalizing environments for Indigenous people. Similar comments were made in the other community dialogue sessions, focus groups, and online survey. Participants identified a wide range of issues, including the non-inclusion of Indigenous cultures and cultural competencies in learning environments; the need for on-campus resources for Indigenous faculty, students, and staff; and a pressing need for authentic relationship building and anti-racist pedagogies.

A central and recurring theme related to the importance of ensuring that Indigenous perspectives and histories are evident and centred across campuses, especially in student programming and curricula. The pervasive under-representation of Indigenous perspectives on campuses was a frequent concern, as was the perception that postsecondary instructors demonstrated insufficient experience with, and knowledge of, Indigenous peoples and their histories, current experiences, cultures, and ways of knowing. There were concrete suggestions for how the university can indigenize and decolonize curricula by increasing program and course offerings with Indigenous content created by Indigenous scholars or educators, introducing more Indigenous-focused courses in every faculty, and increasing opportunities for experiential learning related to Indigenous

Table Conversation. Community Stakeholder (Full Circle) Dialogue. November 4, 2016. University of Calgary. Photo Credit: Riley Brandt, UCalgary.

cultures and traditions. Generally, participants thought that the university needed to create new programs and degree options based on Indigenous knowledge systems. Participants believed that, by making these curricular changes, the University of Calgary programming would be more appealing and relevant to the lived realities and career aspirations of Indigenous students. Such changes could also make the university an institution of choice for Indigenous students.

To create and deliver such enhanced programming in meaningful ways, the data clearly indicated that there needs to be broader hiring of Indigenous staff and faculty and inclusion of community members across the institution. Yet this need goes far beyond simply increasing the number of Indigenous personnel and students on campus. Their contributions would increase the visibility of Indigenous people through their sharing and highlighting of Indigenous stories, traditions, languages, and lived experiences. Participants also said that including Indigenous perspectives in curricula and programming would lead to an increase in Indigenous student enrolment and program retention since Indigenous students would feel represented and have a sense of belonging.

In the early stages of our dialogue sessions, we identified the need for increased cultural competence for all at the university. Participants suggested that there was a need to educate faculty and staff who work with Indigenous students (in both the K–12 and the postsecondary systems). They suggested that faculty and staff learn about the perspectives, histories, cultures, traditions, and lived experiences of Indigenous peoples. There was a call for the university to introduce more intercultural education for staff and faculty guided by the TRC Calls to Action (TRC 2015). Participants also noted that the university must invest in the education of non-Indigenous students, including international students and new immigrants, about Indigenous peoples' histories, cultures, worldviews, and contemporary experiences in Canada. How these cross-cultural teachings are delivered and experienced is important since the goal is to facilitate learning and understanding from Indigenous perspectives.

CULTURAL HUMILITY

As our dialogue sessions progressed, the conversation about cultural competence evolved significantly. Some participants argued that it would be impossible for non-Indigenous people to truly understand the worldviews and lived experiences of Indigenous peoples. Others stated that it was not enough to be "competent" in such understanding, for it would not necessarily change entrenched negative perspectives or behaviours. So these discussions shifted to the concept of cultural humility. Engaging in cultural humility would place Indigenous cultures on an equal footing with Eurocentric cultures and require non-Indigenous people to be prepared to reflect on, acknowledge, and interrogate the values, assumptions, and belief systems of the dominant cultural worldview that they have espoused.

The evolving discussion on cultural humility was closely connected to participants' concerns about and experiences with negative, racist, discriminatory, and stereotypical attitudes toward Indigenous peoples and how these attitudes overtly and covertly permeate the university campus. Participants mentioned that these attitudes could be found among university structures, governance and policies, educational programs, campus media, and faculty and leadership. Participants also suggested that universities are in fact steeped in systemic racism. They said that offering more opportunities for non-Indigenous faculty, staff, and students to

Completed beaded bracelet. Community Stakeholder (Full Circle) Dialogue. November 4, 2016. University of Calgary. Photo Credit: Riley Brandt, UCalgary.

engage in activities that increase cross-cultural understanding would help to alleviate racial biases and perhaps change negative individual mentalities. There was also a specific recommendation to make trauma-informed education a part of efforts aimed at Indigenous inclusion since Indigenous students can be retraumatized by existing university structures and processes. It was apparent that trauma and intergenerational trauma were still parts of the lived experiences of Indigenous students, many of whom were beginning or still on the path toward healing.

Another theme related to the topic of "making campuses more welcoming" revolved around the enhancement of specific on-campus resources for Indigenous students and staff. This theme highlighted meeting the basic needs of students (e.g., food, shelter, transportation) along with providing cultural and academic support for them (from university admission to program completion). Participants suggested on-campus resources such as food and clothing banks, affordable housing options, access to cultural supports, more space for traditional cultural and ceremonial practices, and access to degree programs through online and virtual learning initiatives. They also suggested that additional resources need to be dedicated to recruitment and accessible admission policies and procedures for Indigenous students at the university, including attention to more culturally sensitive criteria and guidelines for university and program admission. Other ideas included promoting and implementing transitional and bridging programs or courses made for Indigenous students and orientation and community outreach initiatives designed for them. Finally, participants also identified increasing online course and program opportunities for Indigenous students, especially those in remote and rural communities.

SOME CONCRETE STEPS

We heard a specific call to ensure that available support services include Indigenous perspectives on healing. Participants argued that wellness must focus on healing from trauma and that healing processes are essential for student and community success. They noted that, for healing to begin, trust must be gained, and once trust is achieved Indigenous people will be more willing to attend postsecondary institutions and feel safer on their campuses. Supporting student wellness was a recurring theme. Participants recommended providing supports and mechanisms that enabled students to adjust to postsecondary and city life away from their families.

Participants also suggested that increased financial aid for Indigenous students—such as scholarships, subsidized tuition, and reduced application fees—would increase their engagement. In our online survey, several respondents expressed the need to increase funding to support Indigenous programming on campus with an emphasis on the Native Centre, now known as the Writing Symbols Lodge.[3]

Participants identified culturally appropriate, on-campus resources and supports and many concrete steps that the university should consider. Following are some of their suggestions.

- There should be increased Elder involvement on campus and opportunities for Indigenous and non-Indigenous people to practise ceremony (particularly smudging).

- Safe and welcoming spaces should be created and maintained to allow for the inclusion, rather than the segregation, of Indigenous students.

- Services should be developed to support Indigenous students during transitional phases, especially during their first year.

- There should be on-campus housing for Indigenous students and their families.

- A climate should be created that ensures positive relationships with campus staff, especially the registrar's office, perhaps through cross-cultural professional development training.

- There should be campus-wide awareness of the many services offered by the Native Centre (now called the Writing Symbols Lodge).

- There should be increased Indigenous cultural visibility as reflected in place naming, arts, and architecture.

The points related to physical places and spaces are important and should be highlighted. Many participants in our dialogues underlined the lack of historical and contemporary representations of Indigenous peoples

---

3   For more information on the Writing Symbols Lodge, see https://www.ucalgary.ca/writing-symbols.

throughout the campus. Respondents pointed to the importance of acknowledging traditional territories, increasing the visibility of Indigenous cultures on campus through art and architecture, making First Nations and Métis flags permanent fixtures, and naming places and spaces after significant Indigenous people and historical events. There was also a call to create more and improved spaces that facilitate cross-cultural exchanges, including Indigenous cultural celebrations open to the public, ceremonial events, and spaces for Elders where Indigenous and non-Indigenous students are welcome for advice and support.

We heard that Indigenous peoples do not see themselves in any of the university's physical spaces. Our data analysis identified a strong demand for the creation of physical spaces in which Indigenous people feel represented, welcomed, and valued on campus. Creating designated Indigenous spaces would amplify the relationship with the land. More green spaces on campus (e.g., gardens, sacred plants) would facilitate connections to nature. We heard many suggestions about how to consciously change the campus architecture, landscape, and art. Some of the suggestions were ambitious, such as the construction of a dedicated Indigenous peoples building to serve as a venue for cultural teachings and events or dedicated transitional housing for first-year Indigenous students.

We heard many comments about the importance of ceremonial space, specifically the space to smudge on campus without having to pay for it or being restricted to the Writing Symbols Lodge. Overall, participants suggested, connection to and comfort with a space or place happen when people see themselves in it. Spaces that celebrate and honour Indigenous peoples include, but are not limited to, amphitheatres, tipis erected in the proper way with the appropriate protocol, art, and Indigenous-language place names.

RELATIONSHIP BUILDING

From our dialogue sessions, a final theme—"becoming more welcoming to Indigenous peoples"—was about the importance of relationship building. Participants believed that, to indigenize our institution, there must be a fundamental commitment to reimagining the relationship with Indigenous peoples and their communities. The participants often framed relational change as moving from transactional engagement to mutually beneficial relations. They stated that services to students must be holistic and family centred, helping the university to gain a better understanding of Indigenous students' struggles and lived experiences in the context of a culture based on collectivism and familial relationships. They also pointed to the need for multi-dimensional collaboration. Collaboration among the institution's units could help to avoid the "siloing" of Indigenous people or perspectives and provide opportunities for departments to exchange ideas, discuss challenges, and reach solutions. Networking and partnering among multiple postsecondary institutions could ensure smooth transitions (transfers) between universities to improve educational mobility and increase the ability to identify and address common challenges that Indigenous students experience. Perhaps most importantly, participants suggested that universities move beyond their historical spaces and domains to work side by side with Indigenous communities, both physically and metaphorically.

Expanding Worldviews

As the Inner-City Dialogue concluded, participants called for the University of Calgary to work with Indigenous communities to move beyond dominant worldviews deeply rooted within the institution's structures and processes. We heard calls for the university to shift models for teaching and learning, with a focus on creating curricula inclusive of First Nations, Métis, and Inuit worldviews, histories, and lived experiences. These calls also addressed the institution's core research policies and processes. To conduct research, participants suggested, the university should be guided by a fundamental commitment to develop respectful and reciprocal relationships with Indigenous communities. These discussions also highlighted core issues, such as acceptance of Indigenous ways of knowing, ownership of intellectual property, the critical role of ceremony, and policies and procedures related to research ethics.

ENHANCING TEACHING AND LEARNING

In terms of teaching and learning at the University of Calgary, the dialogue sessions revealed a strong sense that Indigenous worldviews and ways of knowing were both under-represented and unappreciated on campus. Participants argued that the institution must better bridge Indigenous knowledge(s) and practices with its teaching and learning. There were numerous suggestions about how to do so. Participants called for the university to embrace Indigenous pedagogies, which would require an examination of its current pedagogies and learning evaluation strategies. Other ideas focused on enhancing community engagement to identify common points of interest and developing a staff and faculty cross-cultural education program.

Many respondents thought that it was important to actively pursue changes to the university's curricula. Some argued that these changes must be evident in all courses across the university, not just those specific to one faculty or department. There were suggestions for mandatory inclusion of Indigenous knowledges and perspectives in course content. This went beyond the inclusion of specific historical topics, and suggestions included creating new pedagogies such as land-based learning and ceremony. To accomplish this goal, participants stated, Elders should be involved at every stage of teaching and learning design and be present to support students in actual learning activities.

In addition to the shift in course design, some participants spoke about the importance of having more non-credit learning opportunities available to students, faculty, and staff. Examples included lecture series, lunch and learns, increased cultural events on campus, and awareness training. These opportunities would increase learning about the colonial history of Canada and Indigenous worldviews, practices, and protocols.

Participants suggested that including Indigenous worldviews in curricula would require extensive consultation and collaboration with Indigenous community members, leaders, students, educational leaders, and Elders. They also thought that more content should be developed or led by Indigenous scholars and educators and that classroom pedagogies engage with Indigenous knowledges and ceremonies when appropriate. Participants suggested that this could be done by bringing in more Indigenous guest speakers and Elders and Traditional Knowledge Keepers. Some participants asked about the academic and research backgrounds of sessional instructors and/or faculty members hired to teach Indigenous-based courses at the University of Calgary, implying that some instructors had insufficient knowledge and/or experience. We heard regular calls for the university to focus on hiring more Indigenous faculty who can authentically inform and engage learners across campus.

To strengthen Indigenous programming and curricula, participants stated, the university should implement anti-colonial and anti-racist pedagogies, adopt co-teaching strategies, and provide more opportunities to leave campus to learn (e.g., visiting reserves to learn from community members and Elders or engage in land-based learning). Adopting these strategies in a meaningful way would require involving Traditional Knowledge Keepers (e.g., teaching about knowledge systems) and honouring their knowledge as parallel to that of those with PhDs.

In all of the dialogue sessions, participants mentioned that an Indigenous course be mandatory for all students. All students would therefore learn about sophisticated Indigenous knowledge systems and the history of colonization and its impacts on Indigenous peoples. However, some participants expressed mixed feelings about whether this course would be beneficial. Some indicated that it would evoke all kinds of emotions, including fear of change, and that faculty pushback should be expected and not underestimated.

Finally, participants mentioned the importance of celebrating success among Indigenous students, staff, faculty, and projects. Although their comments likely extend beyond teaching and learning specifically, they do indicate that we could measure success by tracking the numbers of Indigenous instructors and graduates, noteworthy curricular changes, and increases to teaching about Indigenous histories and worldviews. Focusing on success could change educational discourses from trauma-based to strength-based positive perspectives.

RE-ENVISIONING RESEARCH

As we expected, the community dialogues and online survey included many comments about research, a central function of the University of Calgary. Many participants in the dialogue sessions identified the need to reposition, or reconceptualize, research at the university. They noted that research is valid when undertaken with Indigenous research methodologies and that quality research is not exclusive to Western worldviews. They asked questions about the openness of the university to Indigenous research methodologies. We also heard comments that research is value laden and thus reflective of Eurocentric societal value systems with which the university is clearly aligned. Some questioned whether the university's fundamental research processes could change. Regardless, they thought that this reconceptualization of research was an important process of decolonization for the university.

A dominant theme on the topic of research related to engagement and consultation with Indigenous communities and students. Repeatedly, many participants mentioned that university researchers must ask Indigenous students and communities what they want, need, and see as important: that is, what matters to them? Many thought that non-Indigenous research agendas have driven research on Indigenous peoples for far too long and that it is time for Indigenous peoples to determine what is important. This entails far more than just control over the research questions. Instead, participants suggested, research frameworks must expand to appropriately honour Indigenous knowledges, methodologies, and the essential roles of protocol and ceremony.

Notably, an important aspect of respectful research frameworks focused on capacity building. This includes resources such as funding for Indigenous gifting and honoraria, seed money for Indigenous research projects, and monetary incentives for those engaging in Indigenous research. However, capacity building is much broader in scope for the participants. On campus, it is also related to the importance of Indigenous knowledge training for faculty, administration, and service staff. Off campus, it involves ensuring that research processes help to build knowledge and sustainability for Indigenous communities rather than being an extractive process that leaves little behind.

Several institutional and social barriers were identified as key in the process of reimagining research within postsecondary contexts and ultimately universities' abilities to serve Indigenous communities. Examples include the inability of non-Indigenous researchers to make meaningful connections with Indigenous communities, ongoing encounters with systemic and individual racism, micro-aggression, discrimination, social marginalization, lack of funding for community-driven research, and the privileging of science and social science research over Indigenous methodologies.

Participants suggested that these barriers lead to hesitancy among Indigenous communities to engage with outside researchers because of negative experiences. Importantly, many of the barriers identified had little or nothing to do with research. Instead, many conversations focused on the social marginalization of Indigenous peoples, culturally inappropriate testing methods, and a general sense of not feeling welcomed by, or able to succeed in, the university.

Participants stated that a core part of reconceptualizing research is identifying and understanding various research interests. This critical theme emerged in the context of Indigenous people's past experiences with research and encompassed the subthemes of appropriation and the long history of mistrust. Current research, according to one participant, only validates what Elders already know, but it is published as if the findings are new knowledge. Participants also expressed concern about government- and industry-funded research and how it affects Indigenous communities, especially regarding the environment, health and wellness policies, employment, and social programming.

Two ways to mitigate research unwanted by Indigenous peoples are to have Indigenous representation in the research process from the beginning and to ensure that the research will benefit the community. It was clear that Indigenous people will no longer tolerate being put under the microscope by outsiders. Participants described Indigenous-driven research as having an action-oriented framework and a strengths-based orientation that help to dispel the myths about Indigenous peoples.

Alternative research pathways, although broadly conceptualized, primarily involved creating new norms for evaluation, promotion, and tenure and dissemination/publication of results. Participants suggested that there should be ways of disseminating results other than through the publication of articles and that the community should be involved in the dissemination and be given proper recognition. The pressure to publish was perceived as a frustration, and one participant thought that Indigenous research should not be seen as purely an academic endeavour or responsibility and that learning about Indigenous research methodologies should be promoted as an equally rigorous and a complementary academic activity rather than an enforced add-on.

Finally, participants described the processes of conducting and applying research through Indigenous worldviews and methodologies as very different from the dominant research models in universities. They indicated that the shift to respectfully recognizing Indigenous research methodologies is reliant on a strong commitment to community involvement and an authentic, meaningful consultation in research initiatives. Participants regularly pointed to the need for respectful relationship building that begins with Indigenous communities taking the lead in determining what to research, how it is researched, and how the results are disseminated. This was often framed as authentic community-driven research. There seemed to be overall agreement that collaborative partnerships must include Indigenous communities, funding bodies, policy makers, governance structures, and individual researchers. Support should be given to Indigenous researchers, their research should be showcased, and Elders' wisdom should be part of the research process (e.g., the application of Indigenous research ethics alongside university research ethics).

The demand for recognition of diverse worldviews (e.g., ways of conducting research and practising pedagogy and service) touched on other key aspects of university operations. For example, both dialogue participants and survey respondents pointed to the university's process for making faculty promotions and annual assessments. They viewed this process as inherently competitive and based on a Eurocentric framework misaligned with traditional Indigenous values of community and Indigenous faculty members' cultures. One participant noted that the barriers encountered in society are reproduced in university structures, programs, and policies, especially in individual performance assessment and evaluation processes.

As a final note, some participants argued that the act of implementing an Indigenous strategy would demand new and unique relationships with Indigenous communities. Many participants in both the dialogues and the survey thought that Indigenous people should take the lead in developing and implementing the Indigenous Strategy and in how success is defined and measured.

Listening Deeply: Traditional Knowledge

This chapter would not be complete without essential knowledge shared by Traditional Knowledge Keepers at a full-day dialogue held on the university campus on November 18, 2016. They represented a range of Indigenous Nations and diverse experiences with the University of Calgary and the postsecondary system.

Throughout the day, reflective listeners heard stories and recorded reflections on the discussion. A narrative analysis was then conducted on the recorded reflections. Additionally, Dr. David Lertzman, a faculty member from the Haskayne School of Business and a member of the Indigenous Strategy Working Group, contributed his notes and interpretive analysis of the Elders' dialogue, creating an opportunity for further reflection and cross-referencing based on what we heard.

Given the personal, cultural, spiritual, and sacred nature of this gathering, those engaged in the analysis of the information and stories shared by the Elders realized that the analytical process had to be different from standard thematic coding methods. The two graduate students engaged in the data analysis could not move forward with the analysis of the Elders' stories using the NVivo software because of the internal dilemma that they felt. The stories sat for weeks as the lead, Jacqueline Ottmann, prayed and reflected on a respectful process that would honour the Elders' words. Ultimately, she decided to present the information shared by the Elders in a creative form that reflected the fluidity, straightforwardness, and subtlety embedded in the stories. She used a creative analytical approach to express the results of this dialogue in prose. In the poem below, one fictional Elder shared the themes that surfaced during this impactful session. Essentially, this fictional Elder presented the wisdom of all the Elders at this session in a compilation of important truths and teachings for the university.

The Gifting
by Jacqueline Ottmann

There is a strong spiritual dimension, look it's evidenced in all things.
In humility, we speak from our own perspectives, of our own processes of "coming to know" from personal lived experiences.
We do not own the land, we belong to it. The land is sacred, from it we are born and reborn each day. We are renewed. The land provides the laws, practices, and protocols teaching us how to be human. The land defines who we are, so experience the land, nurture that relationship.
"Your body is my body, my body is your body."
Language
comes from the land, it defines our reality, how we see the world. Show respect, acknowledge the language of this place.
Deeply listen . . . heighten all your senses.
"The language has the vibration and the energy of the land, of where it

comes from. Our languages
are in tune with the earth,
this is why there are so many different languages."
Stories tie us to a specific place; they will provide direction . . .
if you listen to the stories, then you will understand.
We have lived our lives, look through our eyes.
We each have a responsibility to encourage, support, nurture, and help maintain
the worldviews of our children, our youth—ensure they do not lose their identity
when they come through your doors.
You can show young people that education is important, how great a culture
is, develop pride in who they are,
but this place, the spaces, need to feel like home.
Our youth, the young adults, need to feel like they belong, then they will be
successful as they maintain
their connection to identity and culture. We can help our young
people by living a good life. Let us be in good relationship.
We all need to be indigenized, indigenize ourselves and our communities.
There is hope.
We have our own pedagogies, our own ways of learning. We know education is
good for our communities, that there is wholeness and humility in learning
that leads to
being fully human.
Experience is learning. Heighten your senses, your awareness, learn the natural
laws of nature, how the past informs the present, and can step into the future to
those not yet born.
Let us honour the different ways of learning, of knowing.
Many are matriarchal societies, our women are powerful beings, we are here
because of
women's strength,
some of their voices have been violently silenced.
We cannot rebuild our nation without our daughters, mothers, grandmothers.
Let us share our stories and sing our songs,
as they were shared with us,
so we can remember.
We hope for change.
Elders, let us teach the young people, we have knowledge to give, let us all
connect with our youth, with people from other nations to build cultural

crossroads.
Let us share our stories and sing our songs,
as they were shared with us. They
are containers of knowledge, containers filled with life, validators and permits.
Let us go on this journey together, in parallel down
the same river, the same path, connected, interconnected, beside each other. We
have done this before . . .
look to the treaties, they have answers.
But let's keep what's sacred to us.
These need to be earned in respectful ways, and this all takes time and trust.
There is a strong spiritual dimension, look it's evidenced in all things. The
Creator's touch and breath are all around us.
We are all related, we are all connected.
Let's start braiding something new together.

The poem summarizing our dialogue with Traditional Knowledge Keepers represents a creative account of their stories and ideas. The title acknowledges the gift that the Elders gave to the university at this gathering. The day was moving and powerful for all who attended the session. The poem honours the Traditional Knowledge Keepers who willingly and generously shared from their hearts. Without their generosity and wisdom, the Indigenous Strategy would not exist.

Transitional Story

FEAR

One of our natural laws comes from a ghost that we call fear. And I guess we were taught, Rose and I, when we got married and we had our children and our parents would say, "Don't scare your children." If you scare your children, that fear is going to split their shadows from their bodies. Their shadow is their spirit. So, if or when you cause trauma to your kids, you split their spirit from their body. And their spirit wanders to other bodies. They know what's right and wrong, but they'll go do what's wrong because they're just following other bodies. They don't have a spirit until you have a ceremony to bring the two together. Then they can make their own decisions and don't have to follow. So that's where the whole concept of fear comes in. The old people told us, "Don't scare your children because you're going to cause trauma, and trauma can harm them." We don't want to scare anyone or cause trauma. So, I would say, I don't want to scare the institution into change, into any of our decisions.

Oral Teaching, Piikani Elder Dr. Reg Crowshoe

6

Creating the Strategy

Shawna Cunningham, Jackie Sieppert, Reg Crowshoe,
Dru Marshall, Jacqueline Ottmann

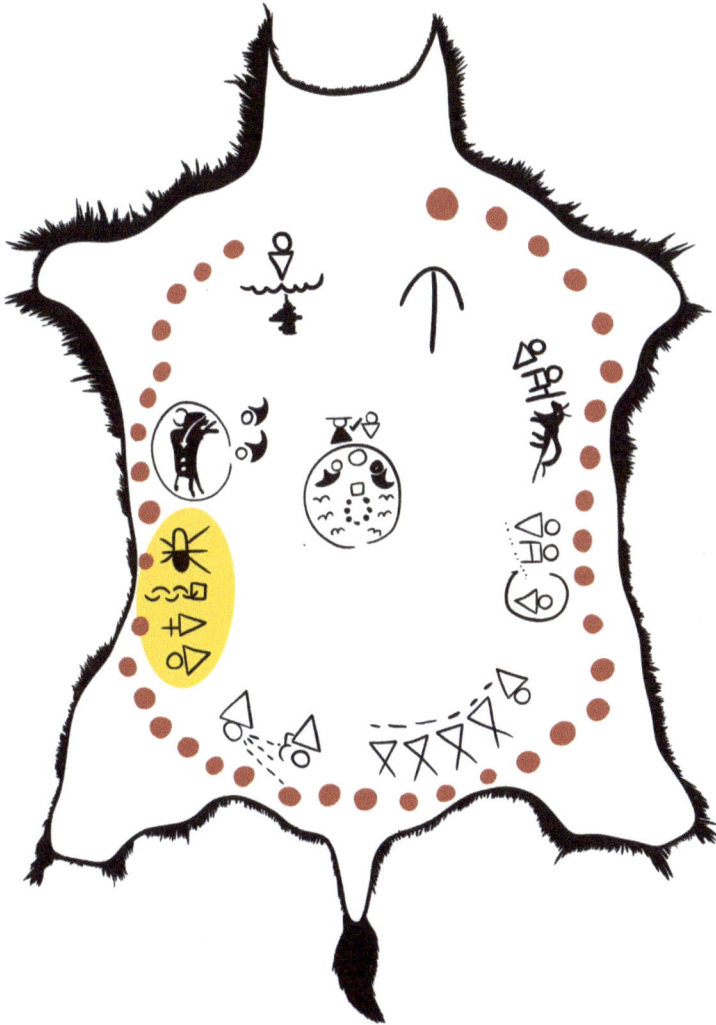

Four Stories

FRUSTRATION

An absolute turning point in the creation of the Indigenous Strategy was during the writing retreat at Fort Calgary. I remember that first day, we had all the information collected from the stories we heard. We had the discussions from the three community dialogues. We had the survey data, focus group data, and information from the internal and external scans. We had everything. Yet we couldn't pull it together in any way that was coherent. And I remember spending a lot of time trying to come at this from very Western angles. A pivotal moment was when Shawna casually started talking about the cycles of trickster stories as pedagogy. That brought the Indigenous side of the parallel paths back into the conversation and propelled the writing of the strategy. And, as we went through that conversation about trickster pedagogy, somehow everything just kind of naturally opened up. I think it was because we again paused and determined that, by envisioning the information gathered through an Indigenous conceptual model, parallel paths emerged.

Jackie Sieppert

STORYTELLING THROUGH SYMBOLS

We hosted a special dialogue with Elders to seek permission to use cultural symbols for our strategy. During the meeting, I recall one of the Elders saying "I'm going to be so happy when I can look at the strategy and not have to read. I will see the symbols and know from the symbols what the strategy is about, what it means, and what is being done." The symbols became a more authentic way of sharing, and the storytelling elements of the strategy fit beautifully within those symbols in a very meaningful way. Our conversations with Elders gave us the support and permission we needed to move forward with the translation of our conceptual model into cultural symbols. We had the great privilege of listening, learning, and witnessing cultural translation unfold in real time.

Shawna Cunningham

MOVING BEYOND FEAR

Early on, we decided to take a trip down south to Red Crow College to meet with the Elders. It was one of the most memorable moments of the journey towards creating the strategy. During that meeting, Elder Andy Black Water advised, "Whatever you do, don't create something that people are afraid of. That is what happened to Indigenous communities." And he said, "Don't create something where people look at us Indigenous peoples with pity. We don't want to be pitied. We have pride, and we want to be engaged. We want to be part of something." We talked about that advice all the way back to Calgary. If we had to pick pivotal moments in the whole process, Elder Andy's guidance would be one of them.

Shawna Cunningham and Jackie Sieppert

RECONCILIATION

Indigenization from my perspective is centring and uplifting Indigenous peoples or knowledges—our ways of knowing, being, and doing. Because of where this knowledge resides, Indigenous peoples must lead that work. Indigenous ontologies and epistemologies focus on healthy and dynamic relationships and continuous renewal. Indigenization is a healing force, whereas decolonization is a collective responsibility because we're all affected by the colonial mindset. We must work together to challenge demeaning and divisive policies or behaviours. I see decolonization as a force that challenges inequality, inequity, and the dehumanization of beings. And both of these—decolonization and indigenization—lead to deeper forms of reconciliation. The creation of the Indigenous Strategy needed intentional and tangible indigenization and decolonization commitments and efforts to make way for reconciliation, a force that embodies peace, friendship, and respect.

Jacqueline Ottmann

Conceptualizing the Strategy

The process of Bringing the Stories Home resulted in a multi-layered, complicated combination of stories and data to guide the development of the University of Calgary's Indigenous Strategy. We knew that integrating all the information into a coherent, sensitive strategy would present a significant challenge. To fulfill institutional requirements and expectations, we anticipated that a written strategy would articulate both principles and recommendations for the university community. We also committed mindfully to an indigenized version of the written strategy as part of our parallel process. Several conversations occurred in early 2017 to determine how to best fulfill these dual commitments.

Members of the Indigenous Strategy Working Group were tasked with integrating relevant information, developing core components of the strategy, and making specific recommendations to the Indigenous Task Force to take forward to the university community. This strategy had to be presented in a manner consistent with other university strategies. That is, a formal strategy document would be prepared and submitted for review and approval through the usual university governance processes.

To begin the process of writing the strategy, available members of the Working Group attended a writing retreat at Fort Calgary on March 25 and 26, 2017. The first day involved a series of facilitated discussions aimed at developing a framework for the core strategy. This process utilized a mind-mapping process to articulate key concepts and linkages among core ideas for the strategy. The group struggled significantly in the conversation since the complexity of the task led to numerous possible directions for and dimensions of the conversation—many seemingly disconnected from one another. The group left the first day of the writing retreat without any meaningful progress toward a viable framework.

The second day initially began much as the first day had. Members of the Working Group, spread across several tables, explored disparate conceptual models for the strategy, yet none seemed to coalesce into a workable model. However, a morning conversation about Indigenous knowledge systems, and the need to transform the university, resulted in a breakthrough that led to an initial conceptual model for the strategy. An animated conversation about trickster pedagogy sparked the necessary shift for the Working Group.

Indigenous knowledge systems tend to emulate laws of the universe and the natural cycles therein. Within this context, transformation and renewal are conceptually parallel to cycles of chaos and order. In this light, "constructive disruption" (Scrimshaw 2021)[1] might be a necessary element of transformative processes or cycles of "universal flux" (Little Bear 2000, 78) in which "chaos is both movement and evolution" and "the field from which all things come into being" (Cajete 2000, 15). Traditional trickster oratory reflects this dynamic cycle of order-chaos-order in which the trickster journeys through cycles of transformation and renewal, teaching us that we are part of a larger cycle of constant non-linear transformation and evolutionary change in an interconnected universe. The experience or journey of transformation might be uncomfortable, unpredictable, and full of tension, yet it reflects necessary flux derived from the natural laws of the universe.

The conversation about trickster pedagogy excited the Working Group as they realized the innate value of framing the foundations of the strategy within concepts of natural law and the inextricable interconnectedness of the Creator to the cosmos, nature (including the land), and people. Early in that conversation, the group also realized that such a framework created an opportunity to incorporate principles of evolution, growth, and life itself. They saw the opportunity to structure a strategy that emphasized conscious evolution over a prolonged period rather than revolutionary and reactionary shifts over the short term. This was not an avoidance of the need to change the institution in fundamental ways but a realization that change would happen through the long and deliberate process of building relationships and partnerships with Indigenous communities.

The second day of the writing retreat continued to play out very differently from the first day. An animated discussion of "four *ps*" focused on the people, programs, practices, and places that would need to be contemplated and integrated in an Indigenous Strategy. From there, the group shifted to discussing core aspects of how universities work, including the "knowledge" of educational and research processes, the daily practices that make universities function, the process of building relationships within

---

1   According to Cathy Scrimshaw, *constructive disruption is "the act of productively challenging inherited wisdom or structure. It supports innovation by opening up the space to replace what we have with what we might imagine"* (Scrimshaw 2021, para. 3).

and beyond postsecondary institutions, and the unique characteristics that help to define a university's identity. The group concluded that an authentic and meaningful Indigenous Strategy should have impacts in all of those areas. The group also recognized that fully accepting these shifts would require an institutional commitment to ongoing processes of transformation and renewal and that such a transformation needed to be guided by a safe and open dialogue with Indigenous communities. As these ideas progressed through the day, the conversation became increasingly animated. It was a celebratory moment marked by music, singing, sharing of food, and a collective sense that we could in fact craft a strong strategy.

By the end of that second day, the Working Group had the core elements of a strategy framework identified and connected to one another. The group created a visual model putting these pieces together and labelled it the strategy's *conceptual model*. It was the strategy's initial foundation, and it served as the starting point for developing parallel paths to make real an Indigenous Strategy for the institution.

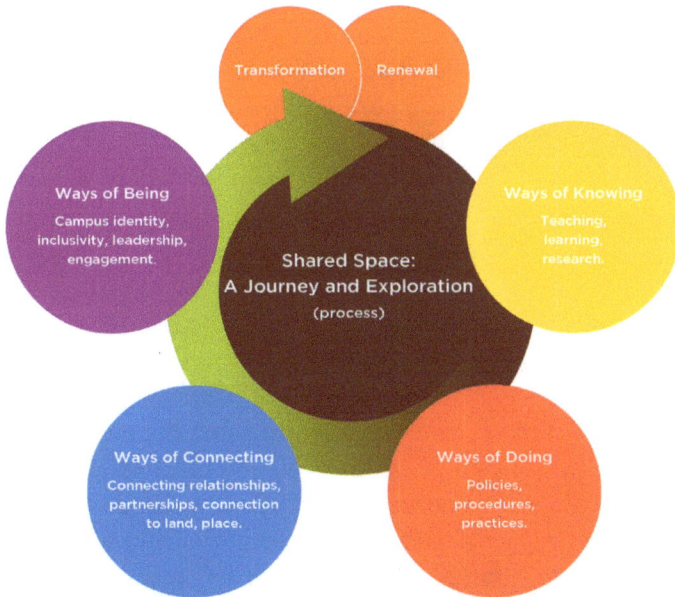

Figure 1: The Strategy's Conceptual Model depicts four large multicoloured circles representing ways of knowing, doing, connecting and being. The center circle represents shared space, and the two smaller circles across the top represent the ongoing cycle of transformation and renewal.

THE CONCEPTUAL MODEL

The initial conceptual model identified both primary principles foundational to the strategy and specific, concrete components that the Working Group believed were essential for the institution to develop. The foundational components of the conceptual model were identified as members of the Working Group discussed Indigenous worldviews regarding how the universe functioned.

This included a discussion on how constant dynamic cycles of transformation and renewal might shape the strategy. From those Indigenous perspectives, transformation and renewal are not only ever present but also necessary and ongoing cycles of life. This is evident in the natural world and all of creation. Change is always evident and necessary.

The conceptual model that emerged during the first stages of writing the Indigenous Strategy was based on what we heard during our community consultations. The model articulated four key areas for the strategy: ways of knowing, doing, connecting, and being (see Figure 1). Each of the visionary circles was considered fundamental to our journey, and each was reflective of the stories and data gathered during our developmental journey. We imagined and labelled these focus areas as dynamic visionary circles. Each circle would be a core focus, a nexus of ongoing dedicated work to understand and implement the strategy. We also understood that each visionary circle needed to be actively engaged in a conscious process of transformation and renewal—addressing challenges, developing initiatives, and assessing success to ensure the long-term implementation of the strategy.

Because none of the visionary circles can be considered in isolation, the conceptual model also incorporated a foundational commitment to process. Called shared space and based on the concept of ethical space, this commitment reflects an understanding that the institution needs to engage Indigenous communities through authentic relationships based on mutual standing, benefit, and trust. As Willie Ermine (2007, 203) suggests, this kind of ethical space depends on a process in which competing worldviews or "disparate systems" come together for meaningful engagement to create something new. Ermine notes that, given the history of colonization, which perpetuates the status quo, the creation of an ethical space of engagement "will be a challenging and arduous task," requiring mutual respect and a true desire to engage in an equitable cross-cultural dialogue that affirms rather than conforms "human diversity" (201, 202). Ermine further explains that an

> ... "ethical space" is formed when two societies, with disparate worldviews, are poised to engage each other. It is the thought about diverse societies and the space in between them that contributes to the development of a framework for dialogue between human communities. . . . The new partnership model of the ethical space, in a cooperative spirit between Indigenous peoples and Western institutions, will create new currents of thought that flow in different directions of legal discourse and overrun the archaic ways of interaction. (193)

Our sense of shared space marks an intentional commitment to create a space within the strategy for ongoing dialogue and active listening. It was Ermine's concept of ethical engagement and his notion of "parallel existence" (2007, 196) that we thought would both fuel and inform our work across the four visionary circles.

The concepts of cyclical journeys of transformation and renewal together with the adoption of shared space resulted in a key realization related to the process of creating the Indigenous Strategy. At every level, we determined that the strategy would reflect an ontology of two cultures walking together on a journey of parallel pathways. Neither dominant Eurocentric nor Indigenous worldviews and knowledge systems could be given precedence. Nor could they be integrated into a single approach, for doing so would create what Dr. Reg Crowshoe calls "cultural confusion."

The initial articulation of the Indigenous Strategy was based on the conceptual model envisaged during the Working Group's writing retreat. For several weeks, we continued to have more detailed conversations about which aspects of knowing, doing, connecting, and being might shift at the University of Calgary and how they would translate into specific recommendations for change. However, in one of those conversations, Dr. Nancy Pollock-Ellwand—the former dean of the Faculty of Environmental Design and a member of the Working Group—commented on the potential use of Indigenous imagery within the strategy. She rightly and passionately argued that, if we were to truly honour parallel paths, any use of Indigenous imagery had to be far more than art decorating a written document. Basing our work on the conceptual model alone would mean adopting a Eurocentric, written model. A more symbolic and Indigenous-centred way of articulating the strategy was also necessary. This step had to incorporate more than Indigenous symbols and artwork—it had to tell the same story in an authentic Indigenous way.

This specific conversation sparked a new and exciting phase of the strategy's development. Decolonization of the conceptual model required that we have a more in-depth conversation with the Elders to seek guidance, ensure that we were following appropriate cultural protocols, ask for cultural interpretations of symbols that reflected meaning within a parallel framework, and request permissions to incorporate them into a truly parallel model for the Indigenous Strategy.

INDIGENIZING THE CONCEPTUAL MODEL

There is much academic discourse on the theoretical concepts of decolonization and indigenization. In light of the ever-evolving lexicon associated with the call for reconciliation in Canada, Jacqueline Ottmann shared her interpretation of indigenization and decolonization with those of us working on the Indigenous Strategy. She suggested that the movement of decolonization is attuned to a cleansing process in which we all have responsibility. In conversations with the co-chairs of the Indigenous Strategy Task Force, Ottmann often stated that, on the one hand, "decolonization is a force that challenges demeaning and divisive legislations, policies, regulations, belief systems, actions, but the heavy lifting to realize systemic change associated with reconciliation primarily falls to non-Indigenous peoples. Indigenization, on the other hand, is a healing force since Indigenous worldviews are grounded in relationality and interconnectedness." Throughout our journey, she often reminded us that cultural resurgence and indigenization draw from Indigenous knowledge systems and languages and should be led by Indigenous peoples. During the Bringing the Stories Home stage of our journey, she also shared that this work can be challenging and likened the resolve required to move from truth to reconciliation, and from decolonization to reconciliation, to a buffalo moving through a storm. Ottmann explained that buffalo do not avoid a storm by finding shelter or veering around it; rather, they face it head on as a herd, as a community, until they reach the other side. The work of co-creating an Indigenous Strategy, through parallel pathways, was not easy, and there were many examples of "jagged worlds colliding" (Little Bear 2000) and ongoing instances of colonial resistance.

To understand the strategy through an Indigenous lens, the Working Group engaged Elders and sought their advice and permission to translate the conceptual model into a decolonized traditional model, based on Indigenous ways of knowing. Historical cultural symbols that reflected the Indigenous peoples of the region are recorded across the land in pictographs and petroglyphs. In many ways for the university, translating key concepts of the strategy into cultural symbols was like being in uncharted waters, with no preconceived notion of what might happen. In other words, we did not presume that every core epistemological element of the conceptual model would result in a direct parallel within an Indigenous system of knowledge creation and dissemination. The cultural model uncovered the complexity of multi-layered, interconnected concepts through an Indigenous worldview.

The realization of a cultural model for the strategy was a critical milestone highlighting the profoundness of Indigenous knowledge, the possibility of transformation, and our collective responsibility for reconciliation. This was an exciting shift in terms of how the university typically conveys, presents, and articulates strategic pillars. Requesting and arriving at indigenization of the conceptual model required extensive conversations with Traditional Knowledge Keepers and observances of specific and required cultural protocols. Guidance by and leadership from Traditional Knowledge Keepers ensured the appropriate and respectful inclusion of the selected cultural symbols. To develop a parallel cultural model, the Working Group first approached Traditional Knowledge Keeper Reg Crowshoe for guidance. After discussing aspects of the conceptual model and the need for an authentic way to express these ideas through an Indigenous worldview, the group realized that appropriate protocols had to be honoured in the process. Permission to proceed in this direction needed to be granted by a circle of Elders who had both the knowledge and the rights to traditional Indigenous designs and symbols.

As a first step in these protocols, three members of the Working Group travelled to Red Crow Community College to discuss the strategy and its cultural model with Blackfoot Elders. In a full-day conversation,

Reg Crowshoe and Jacqueline Ottmann. Elder's dialogue on the use of cultural symbols. April 4, 2017. University of Calgary. Photo Credit: Shawna Cunningham, UCalgary.

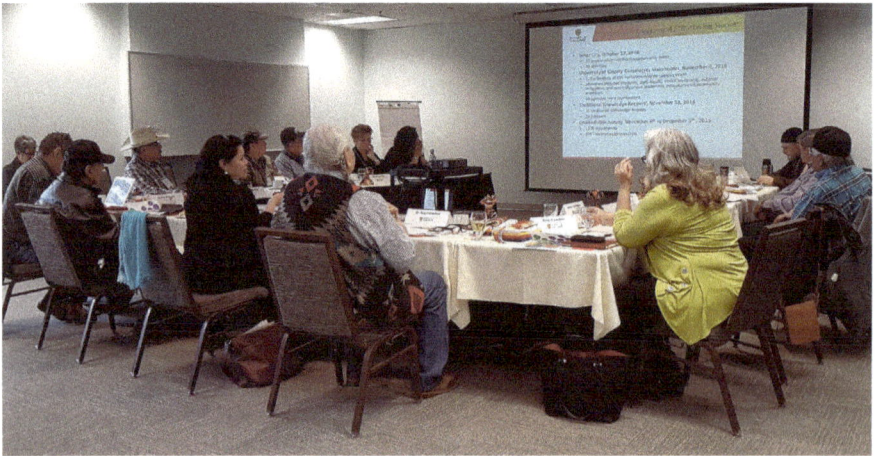

Elders' Dialogue on the use cultural symbols. April 4, 2017. University of Calgary. Photo Credit: Shawna Cunningham, UCalgary.

the Elders supported the idea of developing a cultural model for the strategy. They also offered guidance on the nature of such a strategy and expressed their hopes for the positive impacts that it would have in higher education. After that initial conversation, we invited several Elders to the University of Calgary for another conversation on cultural symbolism and Indigenous design. The second conversation focused on protocols and permissions required for us to move forward with this idea. Members of the Working Group asked Elders, "This is what we're thinking. Can we do this? And how do we do this in a good way so that we're being respectful?" The Elders quickly recognized the importance and power of a cultural model and supported the idea. They granted permission to further develop the model. This was a pivotal and powerful moment in the process of developing the strategy. Some Elders appreciated how cultural symbols, used authentically, could enable the sharing of the strategy's story in a very different way.

The Elders directed the Working Group to begin a process of cultural translation with two Indigenous leaders, Elder Reg Crowshoe and Lee Crowchild, the former Chief of the Tsuut'ina Nation. Chief Crowchild had supported the University of Calgary by creating the Winter Count/ cultural symbols for its Spo'pi Solar House.[2] To support the creative context, the meeting with Traditional Knowledge Keeper Crowshoe and Chief Crowchild to discuss the design of the cultural model for the Indigenous Strategy was held, appropriately, at the Spo'pi House. Chief Crowchild offered teachings about the significance of cultural designs and explained the Winter Count symbols painted on the canvas covering the ceiling of the Spo'pi House. Elder Crowshoe then led an interpretive discussion on the conceptual model for the Indigenous Strategy while culturally translating meaning and drawing parallel symbols. For each drawing, he provided cultural teachings and indicated conceptual parallels through symbolic representation. His teachings also focused on how the symbols related to one another and what they meant, both individually and collectively. From this dialogue, the cultural model emerged, and the story of *ii' taa'poh'to'p* began to unfold.

---

2   For the Spo'pi House, see Chapter 4.

Figure 2: Buffalo Image: Amelia Crowshoe.

The buffalo image (Figure 2) was gifted to the university's Indigenous strategy by Amelia Crowshoe for use with the cultural symbols. It represents the collective journey of developing and implementing the strategy. The rights to incorporate all the other symbols into the strategy were transferred in a ceremony. The process of developing a cultural model for the strategy was deeply rooted in ceremony. The Elders who were part of our journey provided extensive and generous support over several months to guide the design of the parallel cultural model for the strategy. The result enabled the ability to overlay the conceptual and cultural models with one another.

THE CULTURAL MODEL

The inclusion of the cultural model in the Indigenous Strategy is a fundamental manifestation of the parallel processes used to develop the strategy. It provides a non-textual knowledge transfer that mirrors the text in the conceptual model. However, it can also stand alone. In its entirety or in select components, the cultural model can be used to illustrate the strategy's aspirations, stories, themes, goals, and initiatives in various strategy-related documents and websites.

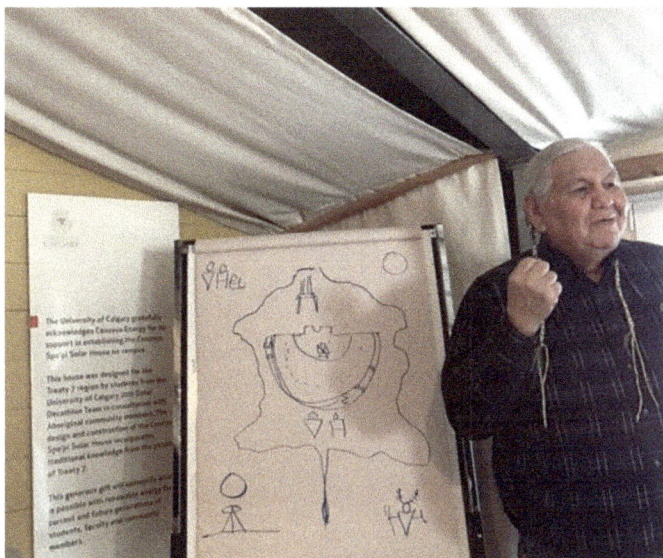

Reg Crowshoe. First rendering of the cultural model. May 11, 2017. Spo'pi House. University of Calgary. Photo Credit: Susan Mide Kiss.

The University of Calgary's (2017b, 10–11) Indigenous Strategy document provides a full overview of the cultural model: "The following cultural symbols gifted for use in this Strategy are reflective of Indigenous pictographs and petroglyphs from sacred archaeological sites in southern Alberta. The symbols are an essential part of the parallel journey toward an Indigenous Strategy. They need to be understood from within a specific Indigenous cultural context that is distinct from contemporary or post-colonial interpretations."

The cultural model represents far more than a collection of Indigenous symbols. The generation of its images resulted from a series of dialogues with Traditional Knowledge Keepers and is inherently grounded in cultural protocols. The final selection, design, and configuration of cultural symbols and their associated teachings were transferred to the University of Calgary through a ceremony led by Traditional Knowledge Keeper Dr. Reg Crowshoe. Although it is difficult here to adequately articulate the full meanings of these symbols, Figure 4 (see page 145) provides a starting point from which to understand each of the symbols from the cultural model (University of Calgary 2017b, 10–11).

Power and meaning are deeply rooted in adopting the parallel conceptual and cultural models, which are visually distinct yet conceptually aligned. The cultural model retains the contextual meaning of the conceptual model and conveys the story of the Indigenous Strategy through symbolic representation. Physically, the models can overlay one another or be viewed side by side, enriching meaning through a decolonized lens of Indigenous symbolism. In approaching the strategy from these parallel ways, the conceptual and cultural models effectively support and uphold one another. Yet the two models do so without trying to merge into a single way of understanding the strategy. Their distinctive assumptions, cultural understandings, and worldviews also mean that each can stand alone, articulating the strategy and its goals in different ways. Together, the two models add deeper layers of meaning and commitment to the University of Calgary's parallel journey. Figure 3 depicts the final version of the cultural model.

Figure 3: The Cultural Model, with buffalo. Cutural symbols designed by Elder Reg Crowshoe.

The legend below provides a narrative description for each of the symbols in the cultural model:

Transformation — (the Journey). This cultural symbol represents "the ceremonial leader or holy person." The symbol reflects that our transformation is a progressive and evolutionary journey, guided by Traditional Knowledge Keepers, and validated through ceremony.

Renewal — (the People). This cultural symbol represents human beings seeking change and renewal. In a ceremonial context, this symbol reflects the process of renewal through ceremonial reflection, leading to self-actualization. The symbol is applied to the university as a living entity.

Ways of Knowing — (Teaching, Learning, and Research). This cultural symbol represents the Sun, the giver of life. The Sun represents knowledge and enlightenment. In the context of academia, the symbol reflects theoretical concepts, epistemology, and pedagogy related to teaching, learning, and research.

Ways of Doing — (Policies, Procedures, and Practices). This cultural symbol represents parallel practices and protocols in terms of Indigenous ways of doing and practicing, including the concept of doing things "in a good way." The Pipe represents validated processes and agreements, and the smudge is a ceremonial process for clearing the path or a "calling to order."

Ways of Connecting — (Relationships, Partnerships, Connections to Land, and Place). This cultural symbol represents the sun, a bundle on a tripod, and the land. Taken as a whole, the symbol signifies respectful relationships and interconnectedness, based on Indigenous epistemology and principles related to communal responsibility and reciprocity. The symbol acknowledges the place (tipi) we gather to exchange ideas (sun), to form alliances (partnerships) and initiate, strengthen, or renew relationships (bundle).

Ways of Being — (Campus Identity, Inclusivity, Leadership, and Engagement). This cultural symbol represents community as a whole, and is inclusive of all human beings and living entities. It also reflects ancestors, present community members, and future generations. The symbol is based on principles of communal responsibility and reciprocity and reflects concepts of respect, dignity, honesty, and inclusivity.

Shared Space — (the Ethical Space). This cultural symbol, an open tipi canvas with the symbol of the Morning Star, represents the shared, ethical space for dialogue — an equitable place that is inclusive, respectful, and exploratory; a safe place to share ideas that help guide and shape the process of renewal and transformation.

Figure 4: Legend, Cultural Model.

Our Core Principles

In writing the Indigenous Strategy document, members of the Working Group and Steering Committee realized that several principles needed to be foundational pillars of the university's journey toward reconciliation. These pillars, listed below, draw from concepts of the ethical space of engagement (Ermine 2007) and ethical relationality (Donald 2016) as captured in a more common Indigenous saying, "together in a good way." Additional key principles, governed by the natural laws of the universe, reflect a cyclical journey of transformation and renewal (Cajete 2000).

TOGETHER IN A GOOD WAY

The Indigenous Strategy is based on a fundamental guiding principle to travel the path toward reconciliation "in a good way" (University of Calgary 2017b, 13). This is an important concept that many Indigenous peoples use, and it refers to working relationships conducted in authentic, respectful, and meaningful ways. Working in a good way requires intention, sincerity, humility, reciprocity, and mutually beneficial relationships. It is a demonstration of commitment, clarity, integrity, honour, moral strength, and communal spirit.

At its most basic level, the promise to work together in a good way reflects the recognition that the power and dynamics that have shaped postsecondary institutions must change. This process of developing truly authentic and reciprocal relationships with Indigenous communities will not be easy or rapid. Instead, it will demand willingness to reimagine core university structures and processes. It will require constant reflection, adjustment, and power sharing in educational and research processes. It must also be imagined as a long-term process of building relationships. In their deliberations, the Working Group characterized this process as a generational evolution—requiring learning, patience, and dedication over many years and perhaps decades.

From this foundational principle, we constructed the strategy document using the concepts of transformation, renewal, and shared space. We did so to ensure that the strategy reflected Indigenous understandings of dynamic and universal cycles—natural laws of change, adaptation, and evolution. Each of these concepts also formed the heart of the strategy's conceptual and cultural models. They are therefore considered integral to the entire journey of reconciliation.

Transformation

As acknowledged in developing the strategy's original conceptual model, the Task Force determined that walking this path would require significant transformation at the University of Calgary. We conceptualized that work across the four core areas: Ways of Being, Ways of Knowing, Ways of Doing, and Ways of Connecting. Although many specific actions and changes would be required across these areas, we saw these actions and changes as being both evolutionary and developmental. That is, the university would need to engage in reflection, formal review, and evaluation as various components of the strategy were developed and implemented.

In considering the kinds of transformation required within the institution, we articulated a series of important changes (University of Calgary 2017b, 13). Conversations about change began by ensuring that Indigenous faculty, staff, and students see themselves reflected on the University of Calgary campus. During our dialogues, we heard that Indigenous peoples were under-represented in our community and that the institution needed to increase representation of Indigenous faculty, staff, and students. There was a need to shift the very identity of the institution to reflect this new, parallel pathway.

Another fundamental aspect of anticipated transformation focused on the ways in which many individuals from the dominant culture need to change negative attitudes toward and affective conceptualizations of Indigenous peoples. This change encompasses both learning about the histories of Indigenous peoples in Canada and combatting myths of and racist perspectives on Indigenous peoples. The need for this transformation was a regular and powerful theme in the narrative data collected throughout the dialogues and community engagement. There was also some urgency in achieving this transformation since shifting these attitudes, values, and beliefs was seen as a prerequisite to developing authentic relationships.

Finally, the concept of transformation recognizes that core functions of the institution—education and knowledge creation—need to change. The institution must create genuine, open spaces for Indigenous stories, methodologies and pedagogies, traditions, and languages. This in turn demands shared decision making in areas that affect Indigenous education and strategies to make Indigenous peoples an integral part of the campus community.

Renewal

The process of developing mutually beneficial, reciprocal relationships with Indigenous peoples will be long and involve ongoing learning and change at the university. We anticipate a constant process of renewal, a reflection of natural laws of the universe. To accomplish such renewal, we suggest that our institution must develop and adopt a sustainable plan for change. It would require clear actions, detailed steps of implementation, and a process for renewed commitment and priority setting. This process of renewal would commit the university to routinely evaluate its progress, shift direction when necessary, and bind itself to the process of indigenization. It is a process that would require designated leadership and accountability, resource allocation, and core infrastructure to succeed.

Shared Space

A final and central commitment in the Indigenous Strategy is based on the recognition that Eurocentric and Indigenous worldviews are profoundly different. This recognition also acknowledges the power differentials evident in the historical relationships between postsecondary institutions and Indigenous peoples. To work through these complex and often difficult dynamics, a process to develop mutual respect, goal setting, and learning is necessary. The process of indigenization would require creating parallel paths for Eurocentric and Indigenous worldviews and knowledges while retaining both as distinct. This would be a process of ongoing dialogue and deepening understanding, of creating "shared" or "ethical" space. The Indigenous Strategy commits the university to the creation of a shared space that will bring Traditional Knowledge Keepers and thought leaders together with senior university leaders for open, authentic, and ongoing dialogue about how to best indigenize the University of Calgary. This dialogue was also thought to be critical in informing and shaping implementation of the strategy.

The Spirit of *ii' taa'poh'to'p*

Within the university, all institutional strategies become living documents that require time, commitment, and nourishment. This is also true when considering strategy from an Indigenous perspective. However, within an Indigenous worldview, the strategy—once named in ceremony—takes on another layer of meaning that includes concepts of holism and inter-connectedness. It has a spirit. It becomes our relative. Since it is our relative, it falls to the university community to take responsibility to care for and nurture the strategy through ceremonial and reciprocal processes of validation and renewal.

Transitional Story

THE NAME OF OUR STRATEGY

The Blackfoot name of the Indigenous Strategy, ii' taa'poh'to'p, *was bestowed and transferred in a ceremony by Kainai Elder Andy Black Water [Aa tso towa] on June 21, 2017. The name signifies a place to rejuvenate and re-energize during a journey. Traditionally, these places are recognized as safe, caring, and restful—and they offer renewed energy for an impending journey. In a traditional naming ceremony, transitioning to the new name is a journey of transformation toward self-actualization.*

> *The University of Calgary needed a Blackfoot term to express the strategy in the name* ii' taa' poh'to'p. *The university itself, that's your destiny, but it's not your final destiny, perhaps to some. Mostly, you go there to rejuvenate yourself, to replenish yourself, to educate yourself. Our young people will go there with the idea and the notion I am going to be going there to do something for myself that is going to impact on my life and whoever is involved with me in their life too. That is taking you to your final journey in life to establish yourself.*

> Kainai Elder Andy Black Water [Aa tso towa]

Empowering the Spirit of
ii' taa'poh'to'p

*Reg Crowshoe, Dru Marshall, Shawna Cunningham,
Jackie Sieppert, Jacqueline Ottmann*

Four Stories

MAGIC DUST

When we're talking about living in the same environment, the bio-ecosystem, we're a part of it. So, being a part of that ecosystem, we need to understand ipisatska'sat *[Blackfoot] or magic dust. Magic dust is an oral narrative about how we came together. Magic dust is like the structure of biogenetics, which for us is an oral natural law. The concept of* íkimmapiiyipitsi *captures the idea of how biogenetics connects to biospecies. It was the whole universe. From the natural law of species, we use the system of relationships and relatives to be responsible to natural laws. We become relatives because we all live in the same environment. The land animals, the plants, human beings, the seasons. And that's why sometimes it's so hard for some of our Elders when they're talking about or sharing stories. They'll talk about our territory, but they won't talk about ownership of land. Ownership of land? How can you own land when you and the land are a part of the environment? We all need to survive within the environment. When you need to do something, or you need to survive, you need to come together as relatives. As soon as you come together as a group to achieve whatever you need to achieve, or whatever we need to do to survive together, then we become relatives. After we come together, everything is your relative, even Napi and Weesageechuk[1] are part of your relatives at that time. Even the snow, the rain, the grass, and the four seasons become your relatives, and we all look after each other. Before going to residential school, I never really heard of the end of the world. We always believed that we look after each other [all our relatives], and the environment looks after us all the time. The process of transformation happens all the time, and it will consistently happen.*

Reg Crowshoe

---

1   Napi is the name of the Blackfoot trickster; Weesageechuk is the name of the Cree trickster.

CULTURAL SOLUTIONS

I have been translating back and forth between two cultures for over forty-five years, hoping somebody would hear me. It seems like I say the same thing over and over again. To me, cultural translation is like breathing because I have done it so many times. People continue to ask me to culturally interpret between Western and Indigenous cultures and knowledge systems to find the parallels in ways of knowing, doing, and being. Cultural awareness training never got us anywhere. We need to go much further and start looking for cultural solutions. How can we look at cultural parallels to explore solutions so we can take on our challenges together?

Reg Crowshoe

OUR OWN TIPI

By the time we got to the final transfer ceremony at the end of June 2018, we were in our own painted tipi. We were experiencing the transformation that the whole Indigenous Strategy Task Force had deliberately sought, talked about for hours, struggled to find the written words and symbols, and anticipated for months. It was so beautiful to be immersed in a unifying Indigenous tradition during this transfer and to watch other people who had been part of the journey come together in ceremony. There were tears. It was so emotional and so beautiful. This final transfer ceremony was a validation from the Elders and signified the release of ii' taa'poh'to'p *to the University of Calgary. The journey and the strategy itself meant so much to them and to us. A deep sense of honour and accomplishment is something that we will always carry along with the knowledge that we were part of making history. The Elders bestowed cultural gifts that will forever be connected to* ii' taa'poh'to'p. *Our strategy is infused with spirit and the blessings of the Elders. In essence,* ii' taa'poh'to'p *is a covenant between Indigenous peoples and the university because ceremony was engaged, and the Creator was a part of the entire process. We must consider the weight of this responsibility and carry it with care seven generations into the future in a good way.* ii' taa'poh'to'p *means so much to us, to the campus community, and to the ceremonial Elders who guided us.*

Grandparents of *ii' taa'poh'to'p*

THE IMPORTANCE OF CEREMONY

I think that hearing the honour song brings us back to that transfer ceremony. It puts us in a ceremonial place. And I would say that, because ii' taa'poh'to'p *is infused with ceremony, we are still in ceremony as we move through this strategy. It is not just an Indigenous Strategy. It is a ceremonial strategy. We have continued with ceremony as we moved beyond development into implementation. We continue to mark our progress through ceremony and are honoured, at key times, with cultural gifts from ceremonial Elders, like the UCalgary honour song, our cultural symbols, the* ii' taa'poh'to'p *painted tipis, and our buffalo robe Winter Count. Ceremony remains part of our parallel paths.*

Shawna Cunningham

A Living Document

The University of Calgary Indigenous Strategy was created as a living document, meaning that we wanted to ensure that it would not sit on a shelf only to be consulted for direction or course correction now and then. The strategy included clear statements of commitment to embed the spirit of *ii' taa'poh'to'p* into the fabric of the institution. As we moved through each stage of development, we intended that the strategy would live beyond those involved in its creation and expand beyond an institutional response bounded by the Calls to Action noted in the *Final Report of the Truth and Reconciliation Commission of Canada* (TRC 2015). The strategy was designed to guide us on a progressive, albeit non-linear, journey toward reconciliation through meaningful inclusion and mindful acts of decolonization and indigenization of the academy, encompassing teaching, learning, research, and community engagement. From the beginning, we felt a deep sense of responsibility to ensure that we approached and envisioned our strategy mindfully, that we did this right, and that realization of the strategy would result in a paradigm shift at our institution. Ultimately, we wanted the university to become more inclusive, welcoming, and accepting of Indigenous peoples and knowledge systems. We wanted a strategy that would thrive for generations to come.

Parallel Approval Processes

Flowing naturally from the process of strategy development, moving toward approval and validation of the strategy demanded a parallel approach. The Indigenous Strategy moved through two different processes of approval and validation in synchronous yet distinct systems. In the parallel process, there was still the significant task of writing a full strategy document to be reviewed and approved through the usual university processes. The writing effort was collective. A small subcommittee of the Working Group and Steering Committee co-chairs worked through April, May, and June 2017 to write an initial draft of the strategy. Equipped with the data and stories from the Working Group's consultation processes, the conceptual model, and the validated cultural model, the writing group used an iterative process, with constant recasting and reorganizing of the material. Several members of the Working Group contributed materials for inclusion and offered feedback on various sections of the final document.

At the same time, key concepts and ideas were tested and debated with Elders and members of both committees. In the end, the four co-chairs took primary responsibility for integrating all the relevant materials to ensure that the strategy document was both coherent and complete. In late spring 2017, a full document was ready for discussion across the university. The parallel approval and validation processes reflected the significant commitments made by the University of Calgary.[2]

Elder Andy Black Water gifted the name *ii' taa'poh'to'p* for the strategy, reflective of places in the landscape that were known as safe havens to the people who were in the midst of a journey—often valleys or sheltered sites close to fresh water. For many of us, this name embodied multi-layered metaphorical meaning relevant to our educational institution. The University of Calgary must aspire to become a place where individuals feel safe and welcome. Through its name, the strategy serves as a constant reminder of what we need to do to redress and reconcile the historical impacts of the residential schools on Indigenous peoples, who were not safe spiritually, culturally, emotionally, or physically in the Eurocentric colonial education system. The name is a call to action, foreseeing the journey ahead and reiterating our obligation to transform the education system. We have a continual obligation to strive, to earn and come into the name *ii' taa'poh'to'p*.

Along with the name, we were gifted cultural symbols for the strategy. Using such symbols, Elder Reg Crowshoe translated the conceptual model, which included four visionary circles—ways of Being, Knowing, Doing, and Connecting—alongside key concepts of transformation, renewal, and shared ethical space into a cultural model. The symbols, representing Indigenous ways of sharing and conveying the storied meaning of *ii' taa'poh'to'p*, were designed and transferred in ceremony with permission from Traditional Knowledge Keepers. As noted previously, we were granted special permission to include a buffalo symbol designed by Amelia Crowshoe to ground the cultural model. The final version of the cultural model was validated in a ceremony deeply rooted in oral traditions. The process of creating and incorporating the cultural model to convey the

---

2   In June 2017, the university was granted permission from Elder Andy Black Water to record two videos—one in Blackfoot and one in English—in which he generously shared the meaning of the word *ii' taa'poh'to'p*.

story of *ii' taa'poh'to'p* was a profound and distinguishing feature of our journey.

From the beginning of our process, key documents were bundled and placed in a pipe bag and transferred to the Office of the Provost as the primary keeper of *ii' taa'poh'to'p*. The pipe bag initially included institutional terms of reference and the Indigenous framework. Later additions included the name, cultural symbols, and strategy document. The provost, Dr. Dru Marshall, then stewarded the Indigenous Strategy through the final stages of formal university approvals, which took place between June and October 2017.

UNIVERSITY APPROVAL PROCESS

Formal adoption of a strategy requires several steps at the university. For *ii' taa'poh'to'p*, the typical steps of approval were completed concurrently with ceremonial validations and transfers. The first steps typically are consultative and, in some cases, informal. We took the strategy to several groups on campus for informal discussions (e.g., the executive leadership team, deans' council, Faculty of Graduate Studies). Each group was encouraged to ask questions about implications of the strategy, provide feedback on its ideas and recommendations, and make suggestions for the next steps. We considered that feedback and, where possible, incorporated it into the strategy document. Those conversations helped to clarify and enhance the structure and expression of the strategy. The conversations proved to be invaluable in identifying hidden assumptions and misperceptions that could cloud understanding of the strategy. Critically, discussions also helped to educate members of the university community on the importance of the strategy.

As we finalized the *ii' taa'poh'to'p* document, it moved through the formal university approval process. This process is cyclical: typically, documents are taken to a series of committees once for discussion, debate, and critical feedback and then to second meetings of the same committees for approval. The University of Calgary has a bicameral governance system, with the main governing bodies being the General Faculties Council (GFC), often referred to as an academic senate at other institutions, which has key responsibility for the academic matters of the university, and the Board of Governors (BOG), which has overall responsibility for the

The presentation of the completed Indigenous Strategy from the Provost to the President at the Indigenous Strategy Launch. November 16, 2017. University of Calgary. Photo Credit: Riley Brandt, UCalgary.

business and reputation of the university. On the academic side, the series of committees included the Academic Planning and Priorities Committee (APPC), the Executive Committee of the GFC, and the GFC as a whole. On the business side, key committees included the BOG Executive Committee and the BOG as a whole. In all cases, the four co-chairs, along with Traditional Knowledge Keepers who were part of the Working Group, presented the strategy. Before it was introduced at each meeting, one of the Traditional Knowledge Keepers offered an opening prayer.

Cultural translation between members of both the university community and the Indigenous community was critical, positive, and generative. Each meeting provided an opportunity for key individuals to voice their support, including the president of the university, the board chair, and members of the executive. This support demonstrated commitment

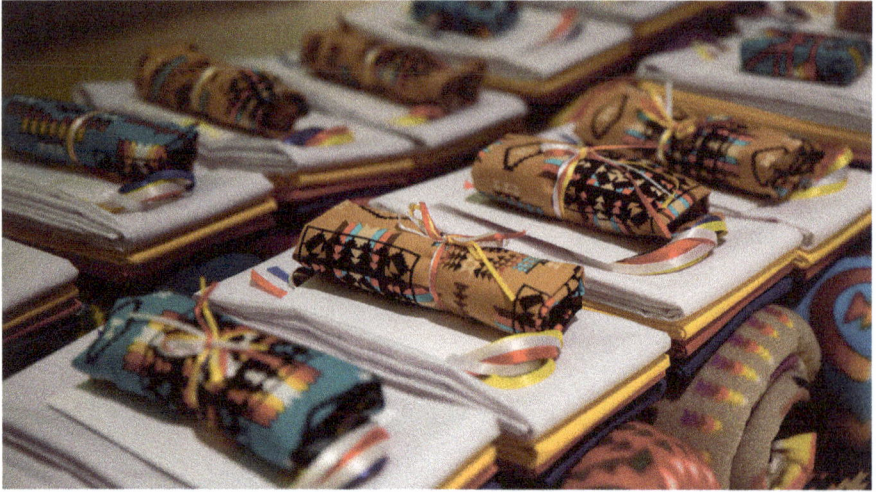

Traditional gifts of tobacco. Indigenous Strategy Launch. November 16, 2017. University of Calgary. Photo Credit: Riley Brandt, UCalgary.

Reg Crowshoe gifting a Blackfoot name to Dru Marshall. Indigenous Strategy Launch. November 16, 2017. University of Calgary. Photo Credit: Riley Brandt, UCalgary.

Aerial photo of the Indigenous Strategy Launch. November 16, 2017. University of Calgary. Photo Credit: Riley Brandt, UCalgary.

at the highest levels of the university. In the end, there was broad support for the strategy, and the process of approval was smooth and enthusiastic without significant delay or controversy. With the final endorsement of both the GFC and the BOG, the strategy was ready for a fall 2017 launch. We were ready to begin implementation of this generational commitment!

The discussion and voting on the strategy were positive, and we received significant feedback throughout the process. This feedback was incorporated into the final document. Perhaps the best example of cultural translation happened at the APPC. In discussion at that committee, we heard an objection about use of the cultural symbol adopted for representation of ways of being from one academic staff member, who argued that this three-character symbol reflected a normative, stereotypical image of a family, with a mother, a father, and a child, and suggested that it be removed from the strategy to avoid such stereotypes. From a Eurocentric worldview, that symbol could certainly be perceived in that way. However, the Elders quickly clarified that this symbol is not a representation of family as suggested. Instead, from an Indigenous worldview, the symbol represents whole communities, all living entities, ancestors, and seven

Dancers at the Indigenous Strategy Launch. November 16, 2017. University of Calgary. Photo Credit: Riley Brandt, UCalgary.

generations into the future. It also represents fluidity, and it is a more holistic, all-encompassing symbol that frames ways of being across time and relationships. On this basis, it remained in the strategy. We also received feedback on the twenty-seven recommendations in the strategy, with concrete suggestions about where specific recommendations fit and what they would mean for work at the university. We learned that we should consult further with specific groups as the strategy was implemented, particularly with the unions on campus regarding collective agreements, to ensure that we minimized any impacts on those agreements.

In hindsight, the parallel worldviews represented in our strategy required a significant amount of cultural translation. Even after the strategy was formally approved through the typical institutional process and validated through ceremony, it was clearly necessary to continue such translation. An Indigenous lens and process were necessary to launch the implementation of the strategy.

Once all approvals were completed, we presented the Indigenous Strategy to the community through a public launch held on November 17,

2017. This event included formal presentations, videos, cultural perform-ances, and a symbolic transfer of the *ii' taa'poh'to'p* pipe bag from the Office of the Provost to the Office of the President, indicating formal acceptance of and responsibility for the strategy on behalf of the university. This key step in our parallel journey included a ceremonial gifting of the Circle of Life Pendleton blanket to the Office of the President, now considered a sig-nature commitment blanket for University of Calgary presidents. A spe-cial blanket and naming ceremony also honoured Provost Dru Marshall in recognition and appreciation of her leadership and support in the de-velopment and approval of the university's Indigenous Strategy.

On June 29, 2018, the university hosted a pipe ceremony to mark sig-nificant milestones in the implementation of the strategy. During this special pipe ceremony, the strategy welcomed the inaugural vice-provost (Indigenous Engagement) and was officially transferred a tipi design and two tipis (one ceremonial and one for teaching and learning) from Elder Reg Crowshoe along with a special honour song by Stoney Nakoda Elder Rod Hunter. The two painted tipis represent the University of Calgary's Indigenous Strategy and our commitment to reconciliation. The hon-our song has become a significant part of our convocation proceedings as well as other important university events and celebrations, including our "Annual Journey" updates to the community. These initial cultural gifts transferred in ceremony—the name of the strategy, cultural symbols and model, tipis, and honour song—are distinct to the university. These cultural gifts and the concepts that they convey have been woven into the fabric of the university in tangible and meaningful ways.

Cultural gifts continue to be bestowed on the strategy to mark mile-stones as we move forward. For example, in the spring of 2021, the strategy was gifted with a Winter Count[3] buffalo robe to capture our ongoing story. The Winter Count is parallel to our annual strategy progress report. That report is presented to the community in the fall of every year to mark the anniversary of our launch date. The report is culturally translated into a pictograph, added to the Winter Count buffalo robe, and validated in a Ceremonial Tea Dance[4] held close to the spring equinox as an act of renewal.

---

3   A Winter Count depicts an oral story through cultural symbols (also called pictographs).

4   The Ceremonial Tea Dance is a traditional ceremony focused on validation of special announcements and vows, with intergenerational ceremonial rights held, led, and transferred by the Crowshoe family.

These cultural gifts and ceremonies continue to capture our collective journey of transformation and renewal through meaningful acts of reciprocity and ceremonial validation. Development of the Indigenous Strategy began in ceremony, and as we engage with *ii' taa'poh'to'p* we continue to be in ceremony.

Implementation

Once the Indigenous Strategy moved through the parallel processes of institutional approval and Indigenous ceremonial validation, we put it into action with an implementation plan that engaged the campus community, collectively responsible for enacting the spirit of *ii' taa'poh'to'p*.

SETTING UP: OFFICE OF INDIGENOUS ENGAGEMENT

The Indigenous Strategy fell under the purview of the Office of the Provost and Vice-President (Academic). To move forward in a good way, we needed to make several critical decisions that would be supported by the university infrastructure. Prior to the development of the strategy, there were few Indigenous leaders on campus, with some pockets of excellent Indigenous programming in faculties and through Indigenous student services. We knew that, if the strategy was going to be successful, more Indigenous leaders had to be present and visible. Thus, some structures needed to be created to bring visibility to and provide scaffolding for efforts at reconciliation and indigenization. New funding was provided to create an Indigenous Engagement Office, faculties began to work with the strategy's recommendations, and an Advisory Circle was formed that included senior university leaders and Indigenous Elders. The journey had begun in earnest.

Within the Office of the Provost, a vice-provost portfolio for Indigenous Engagement was created. It was envisioned to include the vice-provost as the leader, an executive assistant, a director for the Indigenous Strategy, a cultural protocol and special events coordinator, and four areas of focus: intercultural capacity and awareness training, the Traditional Knowledge Keepers Advisory Circle, the Indigenous Students Advisory Circle, and a cultural protocol unit. This portfolio was envisioned to have strong connections to the Office of the Vice-Provost (Student Engagement) and to Continuing Education for both Indigenous Student Services and programming. Once the structure was created, hiring occurred. First, an Indigenous leader needed to be hired as the vice-provost (Indigenous Engagement). Through typical university processes, an Indigenous vice-provost was hired in December 2017 and joined the university in June 2018. The long-standing director of the Native Student Services Centre (now the Writing Symbols Lodge) was appointed as the director of the Indigenous Strategy in November 2017 and served as the de facto lead of the strategy until the new vice-provost arrived in June 2018. A new executive assistant was hired for the office, along with a cultural protocol and special events coordinator, and Dr. Reg Crowshoe was formally named and hired as the Traditional Knowledge Keeper in residence and key *ii' taa'poh'to'p* adviser in July 2018. The creation of the portfolio and the hiring of people also required a budget, which was secured through the reallocation of existing dollars along with a new infusion of strategic dollars. The budget was also necessary for programming.

IMPLEMENTATION STRUCTURE

Creating a meaningful strategy through parallel paths was a compelling experience for those involved. Along with moments of deep learning and enthusiasm, there were numerous moments of ambiguity and self-examination. There was so much to learn about Indigenous histories and worldviews and so much to learn about ways of knowing and ceremony. However, defining and honouring parallel pathways resulted in a distinct and culturally significant milestone for the university. At a fundamental level, the *ii' taa'poh'to'p* strategy forged a new way of working for the University of Calgary. On that basis, we knew that implementing such a meaningful and culturally rich institutional strategy would require a mindful, complex, and engaging structure that remains attentive to parallel ways of knowing, doing, being, and connecting. Implementation of the Indigenous Strategy, prior to and beyond the establishment of the Office of Indigenous Engagement, started to take shape as we prepared to launch the strategy in the fall of 2017.

We knew early on that the implementation structure needed to reach across the institution's faculties and business units and into the multiple levels of the organizational structure to ensure a shared commitment to and responsibility for realization of the strategy. We intentionally created a complex, active process that included both Indigenous and non-Indigenous people who could come together in a shared and ethical space as change makers. We created an Implementation Committee (now called the Guiding Circle) composed of select members of the campus community focused on enacting, tracking, and moving forward with the strategy's recommendations. The creation of the Guiding Circle was quickly followed by the establishment of an affiliated subcommittee structure, now called working circles. This structure, launched officially in the late spring of 2018, included seven working subcommittees, composed of members of the campus community dedicated to specific recommendations outlined in the strategy and focused on enacting necessary and innovative changes across the institution, including reviewing and revising current policies, procedures, and processes; creating new academic and non-academic programs; envisioning new indigenized places and spaces across the campus; increasing Indigenous representation; and reimagining teaching, learning, and research through Indigenous pedagogies and paradigms.

To create an ethical shared space of engagement where the university could speak openly and seek guidance from Traditional Knowledge Keepers, the Office of the Provost established the *ii' taa'poh'to'p* Circle of Advisers. It brought a diverse group of Elders from the region together with select leaders of the university to have important conversations about respectful inclusion, cultural protocols, and transformative reconciliation for the university while staying true to our parallel paths as guided by *ii' taa'poh'to'p*. The Circle of Advisers has been instrumental not only in keeping the university on the right path but also in helping to resolve challenges and introduce cultural protocols for the institution to respectfully engage in transformative reconciliation, moving from a transactional way to a more relational way of doing and being. The journey continues, but as we anticipated it is not without challenges related to the colonial mindset and resistance.

Capturing Progress

In the following subsections, we capture select initiatives that responded to the launch of the Indigenous Strategy and how they affected people, practices, programs, and places across the campus.

PEOPLE

In addition to the hiring of Indigenous leaders outlined above, we increased the capacity in our professorial ranks through three targeted cohort hiring initiatives for Indigenous professors. These cohorts provided new academics with the built-in support of a peer network along with regular support provided to new faculty. We also encouraged faculties to work collaboratively so that Indigenous hires were made in strategic areas where combined resources created an environment for success. Strategic dollars were provided to increase the number of Indigenous postdoctoral scholars on campus, which meant—in addition to the hiring of Indigenous scholars highlighted above—an increase in Indigenous-led research. Finally, there has been a substantial increase in Indigenous-led Tier II Canada Research Chairs across faculties, including Engineering, Social Work, Education, and Science.

To increase Indigenous student representation and create a more welcoming campus, the university reimagined recruitment processes and retention programs through a community engagement lens. We reviewed and revamped admissions procedures, practices, and criteria and created new faculty-based access routes through transitional and bridging programs with culturally relevant Indigenous student supports. We reviewed and refined retention programs and support services to better support and ensure Indigenous student success. Additional Indigenous staff were hired to support new student programs and related initiatives.

PRACTICES

Many of the recommendations noted in the Indigenous Strategy address the need for the university to create a place of inclusion for Indigenous students, faculty, staff, and knowledge systems. Through *ii' taa'poh'to'p*, the university has committed to revisiting and revamping institutional policies, procedures, and practices to ensure consideration and inclusion of Indigenous peoples' practices, protocols, and lived experiences. This has proven to be a daunting task given the scope of institutional policies embedded in hierarchical and transactional colonial structures. The overall intention is to undertake policy review and development by critically examining and revising existing institutional policies, procedures, and practices where and when needed through an Indigenous lens of inclusion.

Ideally, this lens will ensure that Indigenous peoples are culturally safe and not disadvantaged by "normative" institutional structures requiring conformity.

Our approach to transforming institutional ways of doing includes, but is not limited to, reviewing new policies and policy renewals through an Indigenous lens. We have reviewed several institutional policies to date. We have also revised institutional processes to reflect Indigenous ways of doing. For example, our convocation proceedings and programs have been altered to be more inclusive of Indigenous students and cultures. This has meant incorporating the University of Calgary honour song into the formal procession to commence the convocation ceremony and creating space for Indigenous students to add cultural items to convocation regalia. Changes to convocation proceedings continue to evolve as we take one step at a time toward meaningful change.

We have also introduced regional land acknowledgements for all members of the campus community to include at the beginnings of meetings and important events, fostering a practice across the institutions to honour, educate, and pay tribute to the Indigenous peoples of the Treaty 7 region in southern Alberta. To acknowledge the land as a living relative, we have invited ceremonial Elders to lead land blessings to commence the construction of new buildings. These ceremonies are parallel to Western land surveys and groundbreaking ceremonies; however, rather than "breaking the land," the Indigenous ceremony asks permission from the land for the building to be built in that location.

To create space for cultural practices, the university has created procedures to honour Elders as an act of reciprocity through cultural gifting and honoraria. For reporting purposes, the Office of Indigenous Engagement compiles an annual written report, shared with the community during a special celebratory event offered in the fall each year. As noted earlier, this annual report is accompanied by a Ceremonial Tea Dance in which a cultural symbol is designed based on the annual report, validated by Elders, and added to our *ii' taa'poh'to'p* Winter Count buffalo robe. This ceremony takes place close to the spring equinox in March every year as an act of renewed commitment to our Indigenous Strategy.

PROGRAMS

In early 2018, the provost and vice-president academic provided initial funding to establish an annual Intercultural Capacity Building grant competition within the institution. Each project was eligible for up to $10,000 in funding. The key criteria centred on how well proposed initiatives aligned with *ii' taa'poh'to'p* and the project's potential for intercultural capacity building. A similar grant cycle for an internal program for teaching and learning called the Indigenization of Curriculum was also launched through the Office of Indigenous Engagement, setting aside $50,000 annually for faculties and faculty members to submit proposals up to a maximum of $10,000 per year to indigenize program or course curricula. Applicants are required to include Indigenous ways of knowing in innovative curriculum development that engages Traditional Knowledge Keepers, land-based learning, and/or Indigenous pedagogies.

Since the launch of the Indigenous Strategy, similar annual grants, awards, and recognition of teaching excellence have been offered by various units and faculties across campus. There has also been an increase in awards, bursaries, and scholarships for Indigenous graduate and undergraduate students. These types of internal grants and student awards remain important in recognizing Indigenous students and encouraging the campus community to develop innovative programs in response to recommendations outlined in *ii' taa'poh'to'p*.

Cultural illiteracy among the campus community was identified early in our journey as a major concern regarding any meaningful implementation of the Indigenous Strategy, potentially affecting our ability to move forward in a good way. We noted during the Gathering Stories phase of our journey that the campus community was in dire need of intercultural capacity building education. The results of the online survey conducted during the development of the strategy indicated that many respondents—including students, faculty, staff, and alumni—had little to no knowledge about Indigenous peoples' histories, cultures, languages, and lived experiences in Canada. We recognized that there was an urgent need for the university to create and offer more learning opportunities, on both the academic and the non-academic sides of the house, to address cultural illiteracy through new educational programming and professional development. We did not find cultural illiteracy on campus surprising given the educational journeys of some non-Indigenous members of the Task Force. However, related expressions of racism on campus were shocking. Threaded throughout the strategy is a call for intercultural capacity building programs for the campus community, aligning with several of the Calls to Action outlined in the *Final Report of the Truth and Reconciliation Commission of Canada* (TRC 2015).

Since the launch of *ii' taa'poh'to'p* in 2017, various university faculties and units (including the Office of Indigenous Engagement) have created several innovative programs, courses, and professional development workshops that provide a broad spectrum of learning opportunities for students, faculty, and staff. Examples include a series of online learning modules offered through Human Resources, new specialized academic certificate programs, and immersive land-based credit and non-credit courses. We decided, however, not to make these offerings mandatory, leaving the decision to do so up to specific units for non-credit learning and faculties for credit learning. We wanted to ensure that those who engaged in intercultural capacity learning opportunities did so as part of their individual commitment to reconciliation; choosing this route has not been without internal and external debates based on differing perspectives. That said, the Werklund School of Education at the university has adopted a mandatory course for all education students. Additionally, other business units, such as Student Services and the Office of Advancement, have made some online learning courses offered through Human Resources mandatory for all of their staff.

Since the strategy was passed, faculties have developed and launched new faculty-specific bridging programs and/or access routes to increase student representation across the institution, including but not limited to Education, Nursing, Engineering, Architecture, Science, and Arts. Many faculties have undertaken reviews of curricula to create space and/or meaningfully embed Indigenous content in courses and programs. New degree programs, offered in partnership with First Nations, Métis, and Inuit communities, have also been developed. Additionally, faculties have created and launched new specialized certificate programs and immersive land-based credit and non-credit courses (often led by Traditional Knowledge Keepers).

Generally, the University of Calgary has seen a significant increase in research funding awarded to Indigenous-led and -focused research projects across all faculties since the launch of the strategy. The university received a $125 million Canada First Research Excellence Grant for One Child, Every Child in April 2023, with research that "bring[s] together Indigenous and non-Indigenous communities, child health research institutes, education and healthcare providers, equity-deserving groups, [and] local, national and global stakeholders to accelerate outcomes for children and their families" (McGinnis 2024). Key concepts outlined in the Indigenous Strategy, such as parallel paths and ethical space, were core to the university receiving this funding.

Other steps taken to transform research at the university include but are not limited to revisions to research ethics processes to be more inclusive of and attentive to Indigenous research ethics and methodologies and hiring an Indigenous research support team under the auspices of the vice-president research. We have also revised graduate student policies and exam processes to create space for Traditional Knowledge Keepers on supervisory committees and ceremonies in candidacy and oral defence exams.

PLACES/SPACES

The creation of new places and spaces makes the campus more inviting and welcoming for Indigenous students, staff, and community members and pays tribute to the Indigenous peoples of this land. Since the launch of the Indigenous Strategy, faculties such as Social Work, Education, Medicine, Engineering, Business, and Nursing have created new culturally designed spaces for Indigenous students and community members to gather. These spaces are equipped for ceremonies and incorporate Indigenous elements in architectural design, structure, and decor, appropriately reflecting the Indigenous peoples of the region. Additionally, the Office of Indigenous Engagement was provided with a purpose-built space designed to accommodate ceremonial gatherings, staff, and Traditional Knowledge Keepers.

In 2018, the campus architect engaged an Elder Advisory Group to reimagine the outdoor campus landscape through an Indigenous lens of relationality and reciprocity. This ongoing inclusive consultation has resulted in a campus redesign. The university has also identified and created new places and spaces for smudging and pipe ceremonies, where buildings and rooms have either been modified or designed with special ventilation to allow for such practices. Additionally, the university has identified places in the campus landscape where the tipi lodges can be safely erected and has introduced training sessions for the campus community to learn about putting up and caring for our *ii' taa'poh'to'p* painted tipi lodges.

Reflection on Our Parallel Paths

Key concepts and processes embedded in the University of Calgary's Indigenous Strategy, *ii' taa'poh'to'p*, are grounded by Indigenous knowledges and methodologies. The commitment to honouring them through parallel pathways has made the university distinct from many other postsecondary institutions in Canada. The parallel paths followed in the development of the strategy mark a way toward transformative reconciliation, in which Indigenous and non-Indigenous people come together to increase mutual understanding in an ethical, shared space. The four-stage journey framework provided an Indigenous methodology for strategic development that is adoptable and adaptable by, and applicable to, other organizations. Working through and engaging with *ii' taa'poh'to'p* has provided a gift of knowledge and experience, giving those of us who helped to develop the strategy much on which to reflect.

Transitional Story

THE SPIRIT OF *II' TAA'POH'TO'P*

If our strategy could talk, then it might say to us, "Greetings, friends, my name is ii' taa'poh'to'p. *For you see* ii' taa'poh'to'p *is a living document; it has a spirit. It is not a two-dimensional document on white paper or a two-page handout that tells us what to do and how to do it. It has a living energy that we can relate to, engage with, take care of, and help to shape. It is a gift that carries deep meaning should we choose to engage with it, dig deeper, and get to know it better. It has been recognized and validated through the ceremonial guidance of Traditional Knowledge Keepers. It has been gifted with a name, it has inspired the gifting of a song for our institution, it has a story, it has a home, it has relatives, and it has a future. And that future is in all of our hands.* ii' taa'poh'to'p *was collectively created through parallel ways in a shared intercultural space by many hearts, many hands, many minds, with spiritual guidance and blessings from Traditional Knowledge Keepers. We are now responsible to ensure that its spirit is recognized and nurtured.*

Shawna Cunningham

8

Reflections

Jackie Sieppert, Dru Marshall, Shawna Cunningham,
Jacqueline Ottmann

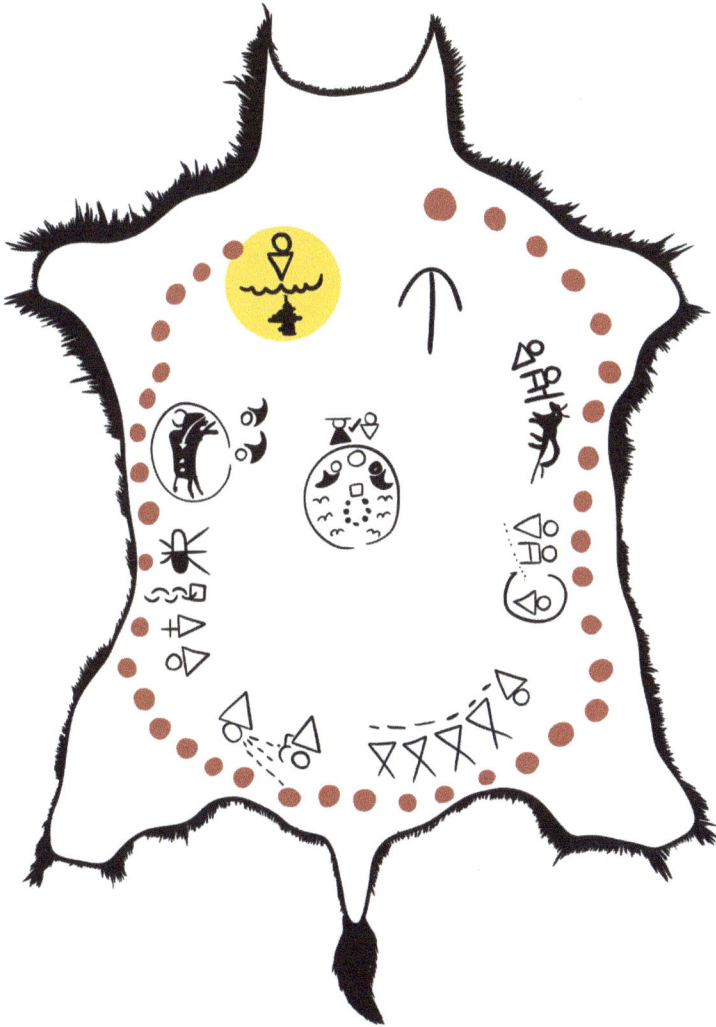

Four Stories

LOSS AND LEGACY

I have learned about the impact of loss, about the legacy of residential schools. As a father, I have experienced the relentless, unforgiving loss of a child. Yet I must say I have no capacity to imagine the loss endured by Indigenous families who have seen their children removed without notice or reason. Families who were not allowed to see their children. Families who witnessed a conscious process of assimilation that stole their children's love, culture, identity, and future. Families who learned their children were abused in so many ways. This is why I am—as a social worker and father—so passionate about our Indigenous Strategy. I am an ally, one who cares deeply about creating hope and new futures for those children and their families.

Jackie Sieppert

WAY OF BEING IN THE WORLD

The experience I gained as a non-Indigenous person through the journey has been profound, and it has transformed my professional practice and understanding of community engagement and, on a more personal level, my way of being in the world. Through additional opportunities to co-create and work in parallel ways with Elders Reg and Rose along with other Elders in the Treaty 7 region, experiential knowledge and practical wisdom emerged. I was fortunate to work on a range of local, regional, national, and global community engagement initiatives with Elders Reg and Rose, Dr. Cunningham, and other university and community leaders. Although my professional role allows me to share this emergent knowledge in diverse professional settings, I also feel a deep sense of responsibility to build upon these unique experiences through my doctoral program and emerging research interests. As I have come to believe, Elders Reg and Rose and other Indigenous leaders welcomed me as a good ally and relative in the hope that I will continue the journey, building greater understanding and awareness among other non-Indigenous people and Western leaders.

Susan Mide Kiss

FEELING SAFE

The concept of safety was also really important in our overall process—perhaps another way to say that is that sanctified kindness was critical. I know I felt safe enough to feel stupid and to ask questions that some might have interpreted as being stupid or perhaps questions to which I should have known the answers. There was a willingness to have that space created and saved, a willingness to show kindness in the approach to how people were treated, that I thought was critical in our frank conversations. And I hope we (those of us at the university) reciprocated and did our part by being open to different ways of doing things.

Dru Marshall

TIME

We felt the clash with the concept of time throughout the creation of the strategy, but especially in the beginning, when there was a strong sense of urgency to complete the entire Indigenous Strategy in six months, in a linear, structured, predictable way. As Anishinaabe-kwe and someone who was raised in a community with rich cultural traditions, I felt this approach would not be received well by the Indigenous community. It would have been perceived as more of the same—a colonial approach by a mainstream institution. Indigenous people understand time as non-linear, and space must be given to allow for the convergence of events to fall into place before a step forward is taken. We calmly wait for all the people to arrive, for protocols to be fully respected, for certain seasons to arrive, and for things to feel right. During the waiting, there's storytelling and a lot of laughter. Learning and relationship building continue during these moments of pause. "Indian" time is not being dismissive of the importance of a person, leader, community, project, or initiative. It is a respectful and anticipatory pause for a "coming together" to become apparent. It is a humbling experience, one that requires surrender, vulnerability, humility, and recognition of the spiritual dimension. Chaos, order, chaos. The Indigenous Strategy had us move through and feel this creative force, especially during times of seeming inaction.

Jacqueline Ottmann

A Look Back: About the Journey

What a spectacular journey we are on! The spirit of *ii' taa'poh'to'p* carried us on parallel paths that unfolded naturally, were guided in ceremony, and were driven by university leadership. We are very proud that on this journey we have committed to creating paths marked by mutual respect, common goals, and commitment to authentic relationships. Together, we will create relationships that benefit both Indigenous and settler communities.

We continue to walk on parallel paths as relatives and to learn from one another. As Kris Frederickson, one of our board members, highlighted in an email to the Board of Governors early in our process to develop an Indigenous Strategy, the *Final Report of the Truth and Reconciliation Commission of Canada* (TRC 2015) provided us with a simple choice: either to do something to improve the relationship with Indigenous peoples or to do nothing to improve the relationship. For us, ignorance was no longer an excuse for inaction. We chose to do something to improve the relationship. Our role also included improving the relationship between Indigenous peoples and the education system. We chose not only to engage in efforts at reconciliation but also to create a strategy that would guide the transformation of our institution into the future. We engaged in this meaningful and inclusive journey with an understanding of the commitment, responsibility, and ongoing stewardship that came with that decision.

Collectively, we have decades of experience as leaders at different levels within the university. Despite that experience, each of us has described the journey to develop the University of Calgary Indigenous Strategy as one of the richest and most impactful learning experiences of our careers. Since launching the strategy in 2017, we have responded to numerous inquiries and presented the story of *ii' taa'poh'to'p* to several organizations, so we know that there are individuals interested in our story who hope to learn from our experience as they embark on their own journeys. We thought that it is important in this chapter to share our lessons learned through deep reflections on our personal and professional experiences, including how the strategy was pulled together and whether it has made a difference.

THE JOURNEY PROCESS

We have been fortunate to be involved in different strategic planning processes, some at the institutional level, others in key strategic areas (e.g., international partnerships and collaborations, teaching and learning, mental health). These processes are cyclical and iterative, particularly during implementation. That is, you start at a place, you know where you want to get to eventually, and you set out on your journey. At various points, you recognize that you don't have everyone with you, or you notice that a key policy or practice has not changed to reflect the new direction, so you circle back and pick people up or change the policy or practice that needs changing. Sadly, some people choose to leave, go in an entirely different direction, not move at all, or stay on the familiar path. With change comes responsibility and choice.

The difference with our Indigenous Strategy is that this kind of iterative process happened during the design phase of the strategy and continued to unfold throughout its implementation. This was partly because we learned how to walk parallel paths, requiring an iterative "checking in" to ensure that we were on the journey together. Through the process of checking in, we took time to get to know one another and developed a deep sense of trust with each other. As our Elder, Dr. Crowshoe, would say, our process included "becoming relatives." In this relational approach, there was the sense of a shared journey with an improved set of relations that would outlast all of us involved in the development of the strategy—which is part of what we ultimately set out to do. Through this journey, we have become a circle of relatives.

The idea of being more relational with each other was different from other university strategies, which typically are transactional and time bound rather than relational and generational. Previous strategic processes tended to last six months and resulted in a document meant to guide institutional actions for three to five years before being updated or shelved for another strategic priority. We soon realized that our initial six-month time frame would not work because, fundamentally, this was about a relationship- and trust-building process. If we were to create relationships in a good way, then that six-month window would have to be extended, and we would have to stop worrying about time. And that is exactly what we did. We needed extra time. A critical aspect of our leadership role was to translate conversations about delays into discussions that leaders at the university would fully understand. Time, so often compressed within university schedules, required understanding from a completely different worldview, one that supported taking the time and space necessary to do this in the right way and in a good way. Thus, the development of the Indigenous Strategy took longer (approximately two years) because it was meant to be a living document that would last for generations to come.

The journey also created a new understanding of the fundamental importance of ceremony for both cultures. There were several moments when, both individually and collectively, we were stalled and didn't know where to go next. In those moments, we stepped back and engaged in ceremony to find a way forward. Every time we did that, we emerged on the other side of the ceremony with a renewed spirit, far less uncertainty, and a collective commitment to continue working on the strategy. Through this kind of intentional spiritual practice, the next steps would unfold and flow naturally, and people would jump back in. Before long, we would be past the blockage and on to the next step. So ceremony saved us on several occasions. Our ceremonial framework and ever-present spiritual guidance from Elders were not just important to the process but also a profound and enlightening core of what we were doing.

For those who expected or anticipated a typical university process, the idea of ceremony and relationality created anxiety and skepticism. As they learned that this would not be a standard process and that ceremony would be an integral part of the strategy, they experienced fear. However, it was ceremony that helped them to trust the process. Ceremony grounded and connected us to spirit.

The degree of cultural immersion in the ceremonial framework for *ii' taa'poh'to'p* offered life-altering moments for many of us. These moments affected individuals on deep individual and collective levels. At the individual level, each person involved in the developmental journey holds a distinct story about what the journey looked and felt like as well as its resonant teachings. At the collective level, these unique, storied experiences contributed to a shared story. To this day, we have conversations with members of the Steering Committee and Working Group who talk about their experiences working on the strategy with great emotional attachment, often leading to tears about the strategy that we created together with guidance from Elders and the emotional, physical, and spiritual journey that it took to get us there. Through the ceremonial framework, and our collective experiences, we became relatives, and the Indigenous Strategy became a shared story of vision, purpose, and responsibility.

This process of developing a powerful, shared story was a highlight of our journey together. The remarkably diverse members of our Steering Committee and Working Group—drawn from every corner of the university community along with Indigenous community members and Traditional Knowledge Keepers—became a committed and closely aligned collective. Many of those individuals became passionate advocates for the strategy in part because of the ceremonial process and spiritual journey experienced. The strategy became a living entity, and by the end those involved in the process would do whatever they could to ensure that it was successful. Their individual story threads, based on memories and lived experiences, came together to form a collective story tapestry, one that continues to unfold and deepen as we gather, witness, and reminisce about our shared journey. The tapestry is remarkable and has incredible energy.

LESSONS LEARNED

Most of us considered ourselves educated, yet the settlers working on the Indigenous Strategy were stunned at our lack of knowledge of the history of Indigenous peoples in Canada. How could we not have learned about residential schools and the resulting intergenerational trauma through our education system? At the start, we were all proud to be part of a country that did not have the overt racism that you might see in the United States, South Africa, or Australia. In fact, though, we learned that the covert or hidden racism toward our Indigenous relatives is much worse in many ways. We learned that we have refused to acknowledge or accept our roles as settlers in the pain, suffering, abuse, and intergenerational trauma that have resulted from the breakup of Indigenous family units. As a result of this learning, we felt a deep sense of responsibility to move forward in a mindful and respectful way—honouring the parallel paths and creating time and space to truly listen to community and take guidance from Traditional Knowledge Keepers.

Related to the above lesson, we learned the importance of the value and appreciation of differences in people. Settlers who were part of this journey learned so much from and about Indigenous peoples, in particular their resilience and grace in the face of so much pain and suffering and their generosity and willingness to share their lived experience and stories of trauma. Their strength of character was something that we could only wish to emulate someday, and we will be forever grateful for having been entrusted with the knowledge to help change how we do things going forward.

Another lesson refers to the concept of relationality. We are so busy with our lives—with our jobs and families and other minutiae—that we have become transactional in almost everything that we do. We quickly learned at the beginning of our journey that a transactional approach would fail. We had to spend time getting to know one another before we could begin to talk about how we would move forward. This took time but resulted in deep bonds and built trust among us. We could all benefit from being more relational in life in general: if we seek to get to know one another, then we will have a deeper understanding of why we think in the ways that we do, and perhaps those relationships will provide more grace, compassion, and empathy during times of contention.

We also learned never to make assumptions about people's prior knowledge. This should not have been surprising given all that we learned as leaders of the process. However, in presenting the strategy to our key governance groups early in the process, we realized that we had to spend some time educating people on critical parts of Canadian history related to Indigenous peoples, particularly regarding colonization and the resulting intergenerational trauma of residential schools. People also needed to learn about the rich, complex, and sophisticated Indigenous philosophies, methodologies, pedagogies, and intellects. This was never more apparent than in our first meeting with our Board of Governors early in the process. We realized that the discussions and exercises that we had planned would not work because people did not have the prerequisite knowledge. This helped to set the stage for requirements for future meetings with our campus community.

We would also like to highlight a lesson related to time. Many institutions, and indeed some people within our community, heavily criticized how long it took us to develop our strategy. However, we believe that the time was well spent given the trusting relationships that developed with our Indigenous relatives. We knew that those relationships would serve us well in the future, and that has been the case. It was vital to take the time that we needed to get it right and to do things in a good way; we needed to be mindful of creating a safe place for everyone, including both Indigenous and non-Indigenous people. When we needed that time, ceremony gave us space in which to reflect, be considerate, and build relationships with one another, loop back when needed, and honour and celebrate milestones. As those of us involved in the strategy development have discussed, we were behind other institutions when we started but have been told that we leapfrogged others by the time the Indigenous Strategy was launched because of the process that we used. The key lesson, as Jacqueline Ottmann reminded us, was that sometimes you must "go slow to go fast."

The teaching offered by Elder Andy Black Water early on in our journey, which centered on fear, was crucial to the development of our strategy. His advice to avoid creating a strategy that induced fear or could be used for punitive purposes gave great pause and helped us to envision a strategy that embraced kindness, ethical space, parallel paths, and transformative reconciliation. At a basic level, that lesson changed our thinking, and we did not call for mandatory courses for students and staff. Black Water also mentioned that we shouldn't create a strategy that evokes pity; rather, it should reflect the beauty and richness of Indigenous cultures. As a result, our strategy was informed and shaped by Indigenous knowledge systems and ceremonial ways of doing. The teachings imparted by Elder Black Water provided insights into finding ways for the university and Indigenous communities to walk together on parallel paths. We had to move forward in a way that placed both communities, and everything that is part of them, on an equal standing. In doing so, we had to embody encouragement and a positive spirit.

Finally, a fundamental lesson learned on this journey was deeper and more transformative than any of us had expected. We developed a keen sense of how easy and comfortable it is to revert to what we know (i.e., Eurocentric frameworks for strategic development). These frameworks— from consultation models to designing and writing a strategy—contain many unseen assumptions, biases, and micro-aggressions. In essence, this lesson was about creating and respecting the ethical space between two disparate cultures. The parallel paths and adoption of the four-stage journey framework naturally bound us to a type of Indigenous ethical framework in which we were constantly reflecting on, rethinking, and validating our stories, processes, and progress along the way. Creating an ethical space demanded commitments to genuinely work with the community and an indigenized community-based model for strategic development. We had to make conscious decisions to decolonize our minds and be open to a different, more inclusive, and relational process. We learned that ceremonial Elders would help us to develop that relational understanding and continue to offer gentle and, at times, firm guidance to ensure that we stayed on a good path.

TRANSFORMATIONAL MOMENTS

There were many transformational moments during the journey to develop the strategy. We were so culturally immersed in the journey that we lost track of the linear timeline, and deadlines took a back seat to the significance of the experience as it unfolded daily. Throughout the process, ceremonial validations from Elders brought deep meaning to the work and gave us the inspiration and support that we needed to keep moving forward. Institutional approvals that came to us one committee after another, as we moved the strategy through governance, brought us such a feeling of invested accomplishment and pride. The constant reminders about the importance and meaning of the strategy made the whole process transformational at individual and collective levels. However, many unique, transformational moments also occurred at unexpected times and in exceptionally surprising, profound ways.

One of the first pivotal moments happened at the public dialogue at Fort Calgary, marking the beginning of our commitment to listening deeply. This gathering invited community members and representatives from social services agencies, the employment sector, and other educational institutions to engage in conversations about the relationship between these organizations and/or services and postsecondary education, with particular focus on the University of Calgary. Several people there perhaps had never imagined that they could be part of a postsecondary system; some might have dreamed about it at one point but never got the support to arrive at a university. During the dialogue, one of the Indigenous participants stated that it was the first time the university had come to the table and asked about their experiences with education. In that moment, we learned to become active listeners. It was incredibly powerful and humbling to hear their dreams and how our society had derailed those dreams.

At that first public dialogue, we incorporated beading opportunities at the tables to make those conversations easier. What we didn't expect is that people who made bracelets would then gift them to fellow participants at their table. This gifting continued into the dialogues and focus groups that followed. Small river rocks placed on each table represented our ancestors. We asked that everyone at the event take a rock, return it to the land, and reflect on and ask about what that process looked like. These small initial steps served as reminders about the importance of cultural traditions and the need to move beyond Euro-centric ways of interacting. The conversations also allowed participants to connect in highly meaningful ways, setting the stage for later processes on our journey.

During the process, there were vigorous debates among our committees about how to best help members of the university understand and better connect with Indigenous communities. We often asked Elders about how to do so. What stood out in those moments was that, as a university and as members of the Working Group and Steering Committee, we had to walk in and say, "This is where we are at. This is what we are thinking. Here's where we are on the journey." And that had to be done with humility. Cultural humility on this journey was so important. And we had to be ready to hear Elders say, "We don't think you're there," or "You need to think about it differently," or "Here's how you might move ahead." So it was that willingness to move beyond old concepts such as cultural competence to cultural humility. We had to be willing to be vulnerable. To us, our strategy reflects an authentic relationship with and a true commitment to reconciliation, because we approached the work with cultural humility. Cultural humility was critical.

In our discussions with Elders, one comment made in passing by an Elder resonated with us. The Elder referred to all of the "square corners" on the campus, which reflected how we had been "trained to think." It's a very structured approach to the world. The Elder added, "We don't think in square corners, we think in circles, and you need to understand what that means." As we continue to reflect on that statement, it's clear that those words reveal very different foundational assumptions about how the world works, how we all interact with one another, and how our obligations to one another unfold. So that simple statement still has us thinking about how to change the ways in which we interact with the world. How do we live in this world in ways that get rid of square corners? There are multiple ways of looking at the world, and we often think that our own way is the right way. However, it became apparent throughout our process that there is more than one way in which to view the world.

As we approached validation and approval of the strategy, a final transformational experience occurred, comprising the Elders' gifts of the *ii' taa'poh'to'p* name for the strategy, the honour song, and the pipe ceremony. These gifts represented a deeply moving confirmation that we were embarking on this journey in a good way. We were acknowledged with the transfer of those gifts, and they reinforced the parallel paths, suggesting that we were finding different ways to tell the stories of this journey and the university. Regarding the strategy, the Elders contended, "We're not just giving it a stamp of approval but also acknowledging that we are on these paths together." For all of us, the ceremonies became incredibly powerful. And for those of us who are non-Indigenous, the ceremonies imbued meaning that extended far beyond typical university committee approvals and endorsements. It was more of a relational approach to moving this work ahead and acknowledging the humanity of the journey.

It was an incredible moment when everything started to come together in real time: the strategy document, the name, the symbols, the stories of how we got there, and finally the launch. The launch was emotional and engaging. It included the transfer of the full strategy in a pipe bag, blanket ceremonies, and an unexpected naming ceremony to honour our provost. The community response to the strategy was perhaps the most transformational aspect of this journey. We did not expect such amazing support from the community during the launch or the outpouring of heartfelt emotions from members of the campus and surrounding community. It was then that we knew we had developed the Indigenous Strategy in a good way.

IMPACT OF THE STRATEGY: INSTITUTIONAL CULTURE SHIFTS

Early in our process, members of the Working Group and Steering Committee began to talk about the long-term nature of our journey. We began to call this a generational strategy. This was a journey that the university would still be on ten, twenty, or even fifty years down the road. When we think about it in those terms, it's natural to say along the way that there will be many transformations and renewals long after all of us are gone. The university's Indigenous Strategy, *ii' taa'poh'to'p*, will still be a strategy with spirit and life. Although it is a generational strategy, different priorities and tactics will be highlighted and used annually. The strategy will need constant attention and renewal as we continue to walk parallel paths. The university must commit to this in a generational way.

For decades, communities in general and Indigenous communities in particular have seen university personnel show up for conversations and essentially say that "We are the experts. We know what we're doing. Listen to us. We'll guide you." In our strategy process, the dialogues rolled out by non-Indigenous people in a very different way. We showed up and said, "We don't know, and we need you to guide us. We need your help. We need to understand, and we need direction on how to move forward." And that was a new experience for everybody at those dialogues, on both the university side and the community side. Again, such a starting point goes back to the notion of humility. That openness, that ability to say we don't know, allowed us to have a conversation that probably would not have happened otherwise.

In embarking on this journey, we knew that creating a strategy that would fundamentally and ideally change the university would be difficult. Deep systemic transformation takes time. It moves slowly and requires many difficult conversations. So we must comment on the presence of resistance and racism on our campus. We saw several racist comments in the online survey. They were hard to read and process. However, what stood out just as vividly were several "resistant" conversations as we worked our way through the university process, comments such as "Well, that's not how we do things" or "We can't do some of those things because. . . ." For us, a big part of the resistance that we heard reflected a reliance on Eurocentric systems without a realization that these systems are dominant or that there might be a different way to do things. A fundamental component of the strategy process was to say that "Things don't have to happen this way" or "We need to reimagine how we do things." We encountered some isolated yet significant pockets of resistance that have continued in the implementation phase. Resistance to meaningful change is deeply rooted in colonial structures and mindsets, requiring ongoing and often difficult conversations. Many of these conversations have led to transformations.

The strategy has inspired systemic changes across the institution. We have engaged in new and extensive professional development opportunities to increase individual and collective intercultural capacity.[1] Hiring of Indigenous leaders to guide strategy implementation and increasing the number of Indigenous professors and postdoctoral scholars have provided both increased visibility and energy to the journey. When you increase the number of knowledgeable, committed people, and you create an environment of cultural safety, you increase the chances for change. This is certainly happening at the University of Calgary, and the impact of the new leaders is felt every day. Many faculties and business units have developed micro-strategies that contribute to and expand on *ii' taa'poh'to'p*. Faculties have responded to the strategy by engaging in thoughtful curricula reviews and encouraging pedagogical practices that align with Indigenous worldviews. Several have also co-created and launched new academic programs in partnership with Indigenous communities to better reflect and serve them and their students, with more programs currently in development. There is a deep institutional commitment to decolonize the research process and honour Indigenous worldviews, methodologies, and ownership of Indigenous knowledge as intellectual property.

Although *ii' taa'poh'to'p* has sparked many concrete shifts across the university, we know that changing institutional culture demands more than just a list of actions. Culture also reflects how people experience a place or organization and how they feel during their experiences. Here, too, we sense a shift at the university. For example, there is a powerful sense of community in hearing the university's honour song—it is highly emotional and inspiring. You can feel the life and spirit in that song, and we are so proud to know that it is becoming part of our institutional culture.

A Look Ahead: Legacy and Hope

When we presented *ii' taa'poh'to'p* for approval at the university's Academic Senate, a faculty member came up to our group afterward and said, "Well, this is all great, but why bother? Why are we doing this?" We have heard versions of that question multiple times. Sometimes it is just a question

---

1   See the end of Chapter 7 for some examples.

about why, and at other times the question is framed in a way that suggests "Isn't this just part of equity, diversity, and inclusion? Why do we have to focus on Indigenous people specifically?" Our collective response is that people need to fully understand the experiences of Indigenous peoples in Canada. We need to understand the history and impact of colonization and reflect honestly on what happened at residential schools. We need to understand all the ways that Eurocentric culture has dominated, marginalized, and assimilated Indigenous peoples in Canada. This is an obligation that we all have as treaty people, and for us at the university part of that obligation is that efforts at reconciliation become entwined with the fabric and culture of our institution.

In retrospect, how we approached the development of *ii' taa'poh'to'p* was unique. It inspired and compelled people to take note and imagine a different way of approaching Indigenous engagement and meaningful inclusion grounded in Indigenous worldviews through relational ceremonial practices that evoke an ethical way of doing and being together in a good way. We hope that over the long term this results in the inclusion of Indigenous ways of knowing and doing in policies and procedures. We also hope that our process serves as a template for other intercultural strategies and initiatives.

For all of us who shaped *ii' taa'poh'to'p*, it represents a commitment by our whole institution. At its core, the strategy recognizes that our relationships and the unfolding of life's events are guided by natural cycles of transformation and renewal. We have tried to build these principles into *ii' taa'poh'to'p*, acknowledging that it is more than just a plan: it is a relational process that involves our children and the children of generations to come. It is a process that recognizes we are part of an inextricably interconnected universe, with countless reciprocal acts of generosity, compassion, and love. We hope to see the strength of these connections woven into the very fabric of the university's identity. In this way, the university will move from being transactional to being more relational. If we continue to follow our parallel path, then we are confident that we will earn the right to be called a good relative.

At the beginning of our process, we were asked which metrics would define success for the strategy. We simply stated when the Indigenous communities see the University of Calgary as a safe and welcoming place for them and their students and when there is a mutually beneficial relationship between the university and Indigenous communities regardless of who is in charge. We have started on that journey together and have taken many steps toward that goal. We hope that our work continues for many generations to come. We hope that understanding becomes embedded in who we are as a university and, as a result, that we become better at understanding individual and cultural differences. Ultimately, we want everyone to recognize that there is a place for all at our institution.

Impacts and cultural shifts created by the strategy continue to evolve as we learn and become better relatives. To document the journey and track our progress on it, there are now annual *ii' taa'poh'to'p* reports.[2] Reflecting on these reports to date, we continue to make progress on this journey. Responsibility for change and efforts at reconciliation have been firmly embedded in the institution. These efforts are not perfect, and we still have a long way to go to become that place of welcome, cultural safety, and cultural humility. We still have a lot to learn about reconciliation, but we recognize that we have the responsibility and commitment to learn as those conversations unfold.

Grandparents of the Strategy

The university has created what many have considered a beautiful strategy, with a narrative that includes not only practical elements but also a good story about our shared history, how we got to this place, and our collective path forward. It is a relational "storied" strategy infused, enriched, and validated by ceremony and grounded by Indigenous ways of knowing, being, connecting, and doing.

As Elder Dr. Reg Crowshoe reminded us in an oral teaching, those who led and were part of the creation of the strategy will forever remain the grandparents of *ii' taa'poh'to'p* and will be invited back to remember, share, and celebrate its progress, success, and milestones. On this journey, we remain relatives of each other and *ii' taa'poh'to'p*. As grandparents, we are responsible to pass on the teachings, to share our story, and to continue guiding others who come into our circle when we are called upon.

---

2   The annual reports are located on the Indigenous Strategy website at https://www.ucalgary.ca/indigenous/about-ii-taapohtop/our-journey/annual-reports.

We have followed up on our collective responsibility to share the story of *ii' taa'poh'to'p* in part by writing this book.

Like *ii' taa'poh'to'p*, the earth is alive. It witnesses our intentions, our actions, and our legacies. The path that you choose must be one of sanctified kindness, for kindness is the heart of reciprocity and humanity. We ask that you walk softly upon the earth. We are all related.

Afterword

MAGIC AND POWER

This is an oral narrative that my dad, Joe Crowshoe, Aapohsoy'yiis [Weasel Tail], smudged and shared. We transfer knowledge and stories with the sweetgrass and the smudge. So this story is told in honour of my dad's knowledge. He was probably in his eighties when he shared this story with me. A couple of generations ago, the Medicine Men were very powerful, and when they practised healing they actually performed magic. An old man, Píítaa i'poyi [Eagle Talker], was a Medicine Man that my dad knew when he was younger. One day he asked my dad to come and drum for him for a healing ceremony. My dad sang the old man Eagle Talker's healing song, and there were some rocks in the fire in the middle of the tipi. Eagle Talker reached into the fire and took out the stones; they were red hot. My dad didn't see him get burned by the rocks. He talked about the power of healing. When Eagle Talker hit the rocks together, butterflies came out. Then he put the rocks in a basin of water, and when the steam came up he took his eagle bone blower, and he blew steam on Máóhk ápi [Red Old Man], who was sick. My dad told me, "I don't see those kinds of powerful Medicine Men anymore." I asked him, "What is magic, and what is power in our language?" He said, "The power is knowledge." The old man, Eagle Talker, had so much knowledge about how to heal and how he would use the rocks and the medicine and the herbs together through his song and ceremony. That was his knowledge of medicine and healing, and that was his power. When he hit the rocks together to start healing and the butterflies came out, and the people in the tipi lodge saw that at the same time (the minute they understood what he said and what he was doing), that minute of understanding is what he called magic, because they all saw the same thing, and they all understood what he was saying. And that is where the belief system and power in our medicines are strong because of that knowledge and magic. When I am talking to people and they understand, at that point of understanding, that is where the magic is. Those were the stories that my dad told me about, when Medicine Men had power and magic. And we still need those people today. We have power and knowledge among our relatives; it's still there, we just see it in a different form.

Reg Crowshoe

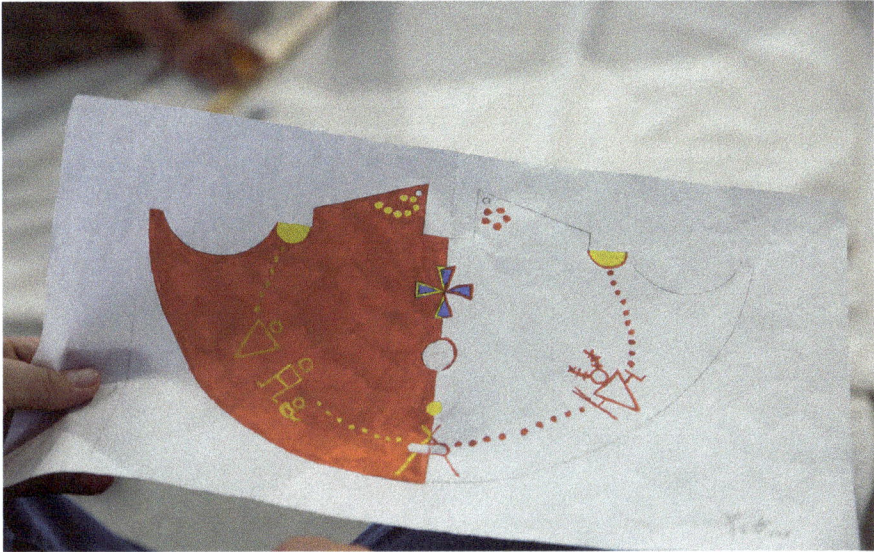

Sketch of *ii' taa'poh'to'p* Tipi Design Painting. May 14, 2018. University of Calgary, Olympic Oval. Photo credit: Riley Brandt, UCalgary.

Sketching the *ii' taa'poh'to'p* tipi design on large canvas. May 14, 2018. University of Calgary, Olympic Oval. Photo credit: Riley Brandt, UCalgary.

Painting the *ii' taa'poh'to'p* tipi canvas. June 21, 2018. Campfire Chats, Elbow River Camp, Stampede Park. Photo Credit: University of Calgary (University Relations).

Special Acknowledgements

The development of the Indigenous Strategy took many individuals who worked closely together for two years. Contributing their minds, hands, and hearts, they have become a circle of relatives on this journey. We would like to acknowledge the following individuals, listed by their affiliation at the time of creation of the strategy.

STEERING COMMITTEE
Dru Marshall, Co-Chair, Provost and Vice-President Academic, UCalgary

Jacqueline Ottmann, Co-Chair, Werklund School of Education, UCalgary

John Alho, Associate Vice-President, Government and Community Engagement, University Relations, UCalgary

Susan Barker, Vice-Provost Student Experience, UCalgary

Reg Crowshoe, Traditional Knowledge Keeper, Piikani, and UCalgary Senate

Shawna Cunningham, Director, Native Centre, UCalgary

Pierre-Gerlier Forest, Director, School of Public Policy, UCalgary

Kris Frederickson, UCalgary Board of Governors

Evelyn Good Striker, Chair, Calgary Aboriginal Urban Affairs Committee, City of Calgary

Jackie Sieppert, Dean, Faculty of Social Work, UCalgary

Florentine Strzelczyk, Vice-Dean, Faculty of Arts, UCalgary

Dennis Sumara, Dean, Werklund School of Education, UCalgary

Roy Weasel Fat, President, Red Crow Community College

WORKING GROUP
Jackie Sieppert, Co-Chair, Faculty of Social Work, UCalgary

Shawna Cunningham, Co-Chair, Director, Native Centre, UCalgary

Brendan Boyd, School of Public Policy, UCalgary

John Brown, Faculty of Environmental Design, UCalgary

Howard Campbell, Calgary Catholic School District

Lyndsey Crowshoe, Cumming School of Medicine, UCalgary

Kori Czuy, Graduate Students' Association, UCalgary

Glen Eagletail, Bull Head Adult Education Centre, Tsuut'ina Nation

Steven Gamble, Representative, Alberta Union of Provincial Employees, Local 52

Alisha Gordon, Indigenous Students' Council, UCalgary

Jeff Horvath, Tsuut'ina High School, Tsuut'ina Nation

Hilary Jahelka, Students' Union, UCalgary

Les Jerome, Faculty of Social Work, UCalgary

Nisa Kennedy, Indigenous Students' Council, UCalgary

Holly Kerr, University Relations, UCalgary

Sheila LeBlanc, Continuing Education, UCalgary

Curtis Lefthand, Indigenous Students' Council, UCalgary

David Lertzman, Haskayne School of Business, UCalgary

Sophie Lorefice, School of Public Policy, UCalgary

Patrick Ma, Students' Union, UCalgary

Sharon Mascher, Faculty of Law, UCalgary

Graham McCaffrey, Faculty of Nursing, UCalgary

Susan Mide Kiss, University Relations, UCalgary

Tylor Pavlik, Indigenous Students' Council, UCalgary

Nathan Peters, Faculty of Veterinary Medicine, UCalgary

Nancy Pollock-Ellwand, Faculty of Environmental Design, UCalgary

Lori Pritchard, Calgary Board of Education

Valerie Pruegger, Office of Diversity, Equity and Protected Disclosure, UCalgary

Phyllis Steeves, Werklund School of Education, UCalgary

Aruna Srivastava, Faculty of Arts, UCalgary

Qiao Sun, Schulich School of Engineering, UCalgary

Dylan Tetrault, Representative, Management and Professional Staff, UCalgary

Steve Vamosi, Faculty of Science, UCalgary

Cora Voyageur, Faculty of Arts, UCalgary

Nicole Wheeler, Human Resources, UCalgary

Vanessa Wood, Enrolment Services, UCalgary

Daniel Wulff, Representative, University of Calgary Faculty Association

CEREMONIAL LEADERS

Andy Black Water

Reg Crowshoe

Rose Crowshoe

Calvin Williams

CULTURAL GIFTS

Andy Black Water, Blackfoot *ii' taa'poh'to'p* name (2017)

Amelia Crowshoe, buffalo image for the *ii' taa'poh'to'p* cultural model (2017)

Reg Crowshoe, *ii' taa'poh'to'p* cultural symbols (2017), tipi design and painted tipis (2018) and *ii' taa'poh'to'p* winter count buffalo robe (2021)

Rod Hunter, University of Calgary honour song (2018)

TRADITIONAL KNOWLEDGE KEEPERS DIALOGUE

Wallace Alexson, Kahkewistahaw First Nation, Saskatchewan

Andy Black Water, Kainai First Nation, Alberta

Edmee Comstock, Métis Nation of Alberta

Tom Crane Bear, Siksika First Nation, Alberta

Reg Crowshoe, Piikani First Nation, Alberta

Rose Crowshoe, Piikani First Nation, Alberta

Patrick Deranger, Athabasca Chipewyan First Nation, Alberta

Casey Eagle Speaker, Kainai First Nation, Alberta

Evelyn Good Striker, Standing Buffalo Dakota First Nation, Saskatchewan

Florence Kelly, Onigaming First Nation, Ontario

Marion Lerat, Cowessess First Nation, Saskatchewan

Warner Many Bears, Kainai First Nation, Alberta

Kerrie Moore, Métis Nation of Saskatchewan

Charles Powder Face, Chiniki-Stoney Nakoda First Nation, Alberta

Virgle Stephens, Bearspaw-Stoney Nakoda First Nation, Alberta

Evelyn Striped Wolf, Kainai First Nation, Alberta

Sophie Tail Feathers, Kainai First Nation, Alberta

Roy Weasel Fat, Kainai First Nation, Alberta

Calvin Williams, Kainai First Nation, Alberta

Bruce Wolf Child, Kainai First Nation, Alberta

Clarence Wolf Leg, Siksika First Nation, Alberta
Tom Two Youngman, Bearspaw-Stoney Nakoda First Nation, Alberta

UCALGARY STAFF
Alicia Clifford, Native Centre
Bridgette Badowich, Office of Indigenous Engagement
Jean-Paul Bérubé, University Relations
Riley Brandt, Office of Advancement
Cheryle Chagnon-Greyeyes, Native Centre
Gillian Edwards, University Relations
Catherine Francis, University Relations
Mallaina Friedle, Native Centre
Keeta Gladue, Native Centre
Cate Hanington, Native Centre
Jennifer Ksionzena, Office of Indigenous Engagement
Samantha Lodge, University Relations
Courtney McVie, Office of the Provost
Sean Myers, University Relations
Cindy Rennebohm, Continuing Education
Sarah Roberts, University Relations
Krystyn Persaud, University Relations
Heather Smith-Watkins, Office of the Provost
Cendrine Tolomio, Office of Indigenous Engagement
Creative Team, University Relations

UCALGARY GRADUATE RESEARCH ASSISTANTS
Victoria Bouvier, Werklund School of Education
Noreen Demeria, Werklund School of Education
Gabrielle Lindstrom, Werklund School of Education
Angie Tucker, Faculty of Arts
Anastasia Johnson, Schulich School of Engineering

References

Anderson, Kim. 2011. *Life Stages and Native Women: Memory, Teachings, and Story Medicine*. Winnipeg: University of Manitoba Press.

Ahmed, Sara. 2002. "This Other and Other Others." *Economy and Society* 31 (4): 558-72.

Battiste, Marie. 2013. *Decolonizing Education: Nourishing the Learning Spirit*. Saskatoon: Purich Publishing.

Borrows, John, and James Tully. 2018. "Introduction." In *Resurgence and Reconciliation: Indigenous-Settler Relations and Earth Teachings*, edited by Michael Asch, John Borrows, and James Tully, 3–25. Toronto: University Toronto Press.

Cajete, Gregory. 2000. *Native Science: Natural Laws of Interdependence*. Santa Fe: Clear Light Publishers.

Crey, Karrmen. 2009. "Enfranchisement." IndigenousFoundations. https://indigenousfoundations.arts.ubc.ca/enfranchisement/.

Crowshoe, Joe Sr. 2008. *Weasel Tail: Stories Told by Joe Crowshoe Sr. (Aapohsoy'yiis), a Peigan-Blackfoot Elder*. Edited by Michael Ross. Edmonton: NeWest Press.

Crowshoe, Reg, and David Lertzman. 2020. "Indigenous Wellbeing and Enterprise: Self-Determination and Sustainable Economic Development." In *Indigenous Wellbeing and Enterprise: Self-Determination and Sustainable Economic Development*, edited by Rick Colbourne and Robert B. Anderson, 10–44. New York: Routledge.

Crowshoe, Reg, and Sybille Manneschmidt. 2002. Akak'stiman: *A Blackfoot Framework for Decision-Making and Mediation Processes*. Calgary: University of Calgary Press.

Cunningham, Shawna M. 2022. "Stories from Inside the Circle: Embodied Indigeneity and Resurgent Practice in Post-Secondary Education." PhD diss., University of Calgary.https://prism.ucalgary.ca/items/b46c3407-93bb-4cf3-ab74-a89ebf9499b0.

Donald, Dwayne. 2016. "From What Does Ethical Relationality Flow? An Indian Act in Three Artifacts." In *The Ecological Heart of Teaching: Radical Tales of Refuge and Renewal for Classrooms and Communities*, edited by Jackie Seidel and David W. Jardine, 10–16. Lausanne, Switzerland: Peter Lang Group.

Ermine, Willie. 2007. "The Ethical Space of Engagement." *Indigenous Law Journal* 6, no. 1: 193–203.

Government of Canada. 1996. *Report of the Royal Commission on Aboriginal People*. Ottawa: Government of Canada.

Henderson, James Youngblood (Sákéj). 2009. "When Learning Draws Us in Like Magnets, Our Hearts and Brains Connect to Animate Our Worldviews." Aboriginal Learning Knowledge Centre, Canadian Council on Learning.

Kovach, Maggie. 2009. *Indigenous Methodologies: Characteristics, Conversations and Contexts*. Toronto: University of Toronto Press.

Krathwohle, David R., Benjamin S. Bloom, and Bertram B. Masia. 1973. *Taxonomy of Educational Objectives, the Classification of Educational Goals. Handbook II: Affective Domain*. New York: David McKay Company.

Kuokkanen, Rauna. 2008. *Reshaping the University: Responsibility, Indigenous Episteme, and the Logic of the Gift*. Vancouver: UBC Press.

Little Bear, Leroy. 2000. "Jagged Worlds Colliding." In *Reclaiming Indigenous Voice and Vision*, edited by Marie Battiste, 77–85. Vancouver: UBC Press.

Maracle, Lee. 2007. "Oratory on Oratory." In *Trans.Can.Lit: Resituating the Study of Canadian Literature*, edited by Smaro Kamboureli and Roy Miki, 55–70. Waterloo, ON: Wilfrid Laurier University Press.

McGinnis, Sarah. 2024. "One Child Every Child." University of Calgary, Research at UCalgary. https://research.ucalgary.ca/research/our-impact/one-child-every-child.

National Centre for Truth and Reconcilation (NCTR). 2024. *Reconciliation through Education*. Winnipeg: NCTR. https://nctr.ca/education/.

Onondaga Nation: People of the Hills. 2024. "Two Row Wampum—Gaswéñdah." https://www.onondaganation.org/culture/wampum/two-row-wampum-belt-guswenta/.

Pidgeon, Michelle, Marissa Muñoz, Verna Kirkness, and Jo-ann Archibald. 2013. "Indian Control of Indian Education: Reflections and Envisioning the Next 40 Years." *Canadian Journal of Native Education* 36, no. 1: 5–35. https://ojs.library.ubc.ca/index.php/CJNE/article/view/196585.

Scrimshaw, Cathy. 2021. "Constructive Disruption—Innovating Health Care: Considering the 'What Ifs.'" *Alberta College of Family Physicians*, November. https://acfp.ca/constructive-disruption/.

Smith, Linda Tuhiwai. 2023. *Decolonizing Methodologies: Research and Indigenous Peoples.* 3rd ed. New York: Bloomsbury Academic.

Spivak, Gayatri Chakravorty. 1988. "Can the Subaltern Speak?" In *Marxism and the Interpretation of Culture*, edited by Cary Nelson and Lawrence Grossberg. London: Macmillan Education.

Truth and Reconciliation Commission (TRC) of Canada. 2015. *Final Report of the Truth and Reconciliation Commission of Canada.* Ottawa: James Lorimer. http://www.trc.ca/websites/trcinstitution/File/2015/Findings/Calls_to_Action_English2.pdf.

United Nations. 2007. United Nations Declaration on the Rights of Indigenous Peoples. United Nations. https://www.un.org/development/desa/indigenouspeoples/wp-content/uploads/sites/19/2018/11/UNDRIP_E_web.pdf.

University of Calgary. 2017a. *Eyes High Strategy: 2017–22.* Calgary: University of Calgary. http://www.ucalgary.ca/sites/default/files/ucgy/groups/Marketing/17-UNV-016-Eyes%20High%20strategy%20document-digital-FINAL.pdf.

———. 2017b. *ii' taa'poh'to'p: Together in a Good Way: A Journey of Transformation and Renewal.* Office of Indigenous Engagement: About *ii' taa'poh'top.* https://www.ucalgary.ca/live-uc-ucalgary-site/sites/default/files/teams/136/Indigenous%20Strategy_Publication_digital_Sep2019.pdf.

Wagner, Verena. 2021. "Epistemic Dilemma and Epistemic Conflict." In *Epistemic Duties: New Arguments, New Angles*, edited by Scott Stapleford and Kevin McCain. New York: Routledge.

Wilson, Shawn. 2008. *Research Is Ceremony: Indigenous Research Methods.* Winnipeg: Fernwood Publishing.

About the Authors

Grandparents of *ii' taa'poh'to'p*

Within that oral Blackfoot Piikani system of making relatives, I am acknowledged as a ceremonialist who will run the Sun Dances, or the Thunder Pipe ceremonies, or other ceremonies, such as those of the Brave Dog Society. I've also had the privilege of caring for a few bundles that I've transferred on to new owners. Once you've transferred on a bundle, you become a ceremonial grandparent to that individual or to that group of individuals. And then you're recognized as an Elder, according to our traditional criteria. But I would call myself a ceremonial grandparent. In our traditional community, that's how I'm recognized. And I'm also a teacher, and I'm still facilitating our ceremonies.

Reg Crowshoe

After completion of the Indigenous Strategy, Elder Reg Crowshoe bestowed the honour and significant responsibility of grandparent or Elder of *ii' taa'poh'to'p* on the four co-chairs: Dru Marshall, Jacqueline Ottmann (Steering Committee co-chairs), Shawna Cunningham, and Jackie Sieppert (Working Group co-chairs). As Kim Anderson writes, "one cannot overstate the role of elders in traditional Indigenous societies" (2011, 126). Elders are respected because they "are teachers of history, traditions, language, and philosophy. They are also keepers of the law, nurturers, advisors and leaders in ceremonial practices" (Mosôm Danny Musqua, quoted in Anderson 2011, 126). Elders have earned authority and responsibility for "generational exchange: elder generations pass on power and knowledge toward life to younger generations" (Anderson 2011, 127) since they have gained deep understanding of *bimaadiziwin* (life) or *mino-bimaadiziwin* (good life). In many Indigenous circles, grandparents have corresponding responsibilities.

The gift bestowed to us by Elder Crowshoe was also a tremendous responsibility. We are the keepers of the *ii' taa'poh'to'p* story, its origin, growth, and release. As we do in this book, we have shared this story from our perspectives and provided details of the spirit, intent, and actions that led to the formal strategy document. Our responsibility as grandparents is to nurture and advise when called upon, even from our positions and places outside the University of Calgary. Through *ii' taa'poh'to'p*, we will always be connected to this university.

We accepted the responsibility that Elder Crowshoe gave each of us by stating the authorship of this book as "the Grandparents of *ii' taa'poh'to'p*." This collective authorship also recognizes the difficulty that we had with "Western" practices of publication related to multiple authorship and the seeming erasure of some of the authors by the application of "et al." in citations. This goes against Indigenous ways of being, knowing, and doing and contributes to the colonial-directed and -driven lived experiences of Indigenous peoples in which erasing and silencing were primary goals. Authorship order is given in the chapters, but this also was not an easy process for us. As *ii' taa'poh'to'p* inspires systemic change, perhaps the declaration of issues such as authorship will lead to creative solutions.

Reg Crowshoe

My name is Reg Crowshoe. My Blackfoot name is Awakaaseena, which is Deer Chief in our language, and that was my grandfather's name. I'm from the Piikani Nation in southern Alberta. My father is Joe Crowshoe or Aapohsoy'yiis [Weasel Tail]. Aapohsoy'yiis was an Elder and a Bundle Keeper from the Piikani Nation for many years. He held on to the Short Thunder Medicine Pipe Bundle, and he ran the Sun Dances and was instrumental in bringing back the Brave Dog Society and the Chickadee Society. I think without his teachings we would have lost a lot of our culture. I'm happy to have been exposed to his teachings. He was over one hundred years old when he passed away. So I benefited from his knowledge. My mother's side of the family was from the Nez Perce Nation in Idaho, and Chief Joseph, who fought the US Army all the way up to the Canadian border and brought his people's children to the Canadian side; the children were taken and hidden by the Piikani. When the Indian Agent asked who this new group of people claiming to be Piikani were, our people gave them the only name they could think of that related to the children; they gave them the last name of Warrior. So today we still have the family name of Warrior in my mother's family.

For white man's knowledge, I was brought to the St. Cypriot Anglican Residential School on the Piikani Nation when I was young. But before I went to school, I spoke my language, and I believed in my grandmothers' and grandfathers' ways. When I went to residential school, I was totally lost because the written system did not reflect my oral belief system in any way. But I have to admit that I got an education through residential school. It wasn't good, but I learned how to read and write, and that's still helping me today. I completed my high school, and I went to the University of Calgary for a while, but we were still being monitored by an Indian Agent. My mind was focused on freedom and not education at that time, so I felt like I needed to run away from university. Later I joined the RCMP. Once I was stationed in Pincher Creek, I moved back to my community and started working with the Piikani Nation. All along, I continued to learn from looking after the old people. I started working with Indigenous governance and cultural processes. I travelled extensively and met with Indigenous peoples around the globe and learned about common hardships and traditional governance structures. I decided to write a book to capture oral governance practices and parallels. I co-authored a book published by the University of Calgary Press titled Akak'stiman: *A Blackfoot Framework for Decision-Making and Mediation Processes* (Crowshoe and Manneschmidt 2002). I have contributed to numerous other publications and video/film projects that include the Piikani perspective on justice and sentencing circles, science, sustainability, and organizational strategies. In 2001, I received an honorary Doctor of Laws degree from the University of Calgary.

I had a chance to learn and understand both written and oral systems and to find the parallels between the two, allowing me to extract oral systems and tools that we need to share with and teach our young people so that they can understand and carry on our culture. My passion is cultural preservation, protection, and renewal of our ways. I have worked with many organizations on cultural interpretation/translation to find parallels to transform systems and make relatives.

Dru Marshall

My name is Dru Marshall. I am also known as Nipomaki Innskii Aki [Chickadee Song Woman], a name that Elder Reg Crowshoe gifted to me during the launch of our Indigenous Strategy. I was the provost and vice-president academic for the University of Calgary when we developed the strategy and during the first years of its implementation, and I served as the co-chair of the Steering Committee for the strategy. I am an educator, a leader, coach, daughter, wife, sister, and an aunt. I am originally from Winnipeg and have spent almost all of my life on the beautiful big-sky country of the Canadian prairies. I was fortunate to have parents and grandparents who encouraged me to do and be anything that I wanted to do and be, even when many others in society did not believe that young girls had multiple options. My mother was a nurse and taught me to value and appreciate the differences in people regardless of nationality, race, gender, colour, sexuality, or any other defining characteristic. My father was an undercover detective with the Winnipeg Police Force, and I learned early on how disadvantages in upbringing can have consequences later in life.

The development of *ii' taa'poh'to'p* was a transformative experience for me. I was in awe of the dedication and commitment of our co-chairs and Traditional Knowledge Keepers to reconciliation and indigenization efforts. They served, and continue to serve, as excellent role models for me and others. Learning is important to me, and I learned many lessons during the development of our Indigenous Strategy. I consider myself an educated person but was stunned by my lack of knowledge of Canadian history, particularly as it relates to Indigenous peoples. How could I not have learned about residential schools and the resulting intergenerational trauma in history classes? I recall how proud I used to feel about being part of a country that did not have the overt racism that you might see in other countries. In fact, I learned that the covert racism toward our Indigenous relatives is much worse in many ways. Until recently, Canadians have refused to acknowledge the impacts of colonization on Indigenous peoples and accept our roles in reconciliation to address the pain, suffering, abuse, and intergenerational trauma that have resulted. As a result of the learning acquired developing this strategy, I feel a deep sense of responsibility to support our journey together as we walk parallel paths in mutual respect and a good way.

Jacqueline Ottmann

Aniin nidinowaymahginuk (Greetings, my relations). I am also known as Mizowaykomigukpaypomwayotung [Thunder Rolling Over a Large Landscape] (gifted to me as an infant by Elder Silverquill), and I am Anishinaabekwe from Treaty 4, nochikinnozāoning (Fishing Lake First Nation in Saskatchewan). The late Chief Allan Paquachan and Marjorie Paquachan (Kayseas) would address me as *nitanis* (daughter). Henry and Marjorie (Kitikaywinnie) Kayseas and Andrew and Helen (Desjarlais) Paquachan would call me *nōhsis* (granddaughter). I grew up with five younger brothers (*ničimēnsuk*) (Fenton, Keith, Giles, Jeffrey, and Kevin) who identify themselves as providers, or hunters, for our community.

My grandparents had a lifetime of education but experienced varying degrees of schooling. *Nimosôm* (my paternal grandfather) Andrew spent many years attending Gordon's and Elkhorn Indian Residential Schools, whereas my *nookoo* (maternal grandmother) Marjorie did not attend these schools and thus had a strong connection to the *nakawe* (Saulteaux/ Plains Ojibwe) language, culture, and traditional practices. I spent a lot of time with my *nookoo* Marjorie in my early years. I remember being in the garden with her, walking through the bush while she picked medicines, and responding to her request to sit still while the thunderbirds moved past us. Now I have many responsibilities: mother of two gifted young adults (Cole and Shawkay), wife/partner of Pat, daughter, sister, auntie, leader, and teacher. These responsibilities are informed by Anishinaabe ways of being, knowing, and doing.

I have always valued education, largely because my parents valued and were passionate about it. Education, from this perspective, would include schooling in a provincial system in addition to the learning that comes from the everyday lessons of life. Prior to entering Kindergarten at age four, I spoke only Saulteaux, as did most everyone in my community. My parents spoke English only when required. I remember being not only nourished by, and feeling strongly connected to, my family and community but also perplexed and concerned by the challenging realities that we, as First Nations Peoples, encountered on a recurring basis.

I earned my Bachelor of Education degree in May 1989 from the University of Calgary and then went back to the university in 2004 as a faculty member in the Faculty of Education (now the Werklund School of Education). I spent thirteen years there teaching, researching, publishing, establishing national and international scholarly networks as a faculty member, and undertaking various leadership roles. Co-chairing the Steering Committee with Provost Dru Marshall and working with co-chairs Shawna Cunningham and Jackie Sieppert, Elders Reg and Rose Crowshoe and other inspiring Elders, and the committed organizing teams and volunteers to bring *ii' taa'poh'to'p* into reality were pivotal experiences for me. I will be forever grateful for this opportunity.

Shawna Cunningham

My name is Shawna Cunningham. I am also known as Mai'stóó pi'kssakii [Crow Spirit Woman], a name gifted to me in 2014 by Elders Reg and Rose Crowshoe, whom I have been blessed and honoured to know since childhood. I am Métis, with historical and ancestral ties to the Edmonton (North Saskatchewan) River Valley, St. Albert, Lac Ste. Anne, and the Lesser Slave Lake region. I had the great privilege of being born and raised in the heart of Blackfoot country—in southwestern Alberta, along the foothills and the shadows of the Rocky Mountains—a landscape that I love and a place that is forever part of my being.

My Métis-Cree-settler heritage and the place in which I was born and raised are part of my cultural, intercultural, and intergenerational identity. I come from a family of educators. I have devoted my career to Indigenous inclusion in postsecondary education systems and my heart to helping create a learning environment in which Indigenous people feel welcome, safe, and respected. I envision universities as places where Indigenous students, communities, and knowledge systems can thrive without interference or prejudice.

I have a long history with the University of Calgary. In 2000, I was hired as the director of the Native (Student) Centre (now the Writing Symbols Lodge) and served in that role for seventeen years. In late 2015, I was appointed by the Office of the Provost to the Indigenous Task Force Steering Committee and was one of the co-chairs of the Working Group that helped to develop the University of Calgary's Indigenous Strategy. In 2017, shortly after the launch of the strategy, I was appointed as the director of the strategy and have continued to work on the implementation of *ii' taa'poh'to'p*.

Working together on the development of the Indigenous Strategy was a profound collective journey and continues to stand out as one of the highlights of my career in postsecondary education. I remain grateful to the university for giving me the opportunity to be involved and for providing us with the space and time we needed to co-create this strategy in a good and respectful way. The spirit of *ii' taa'poh'to'p* carried us on parallel paths that unfolded naturally, were guided through ceremony, and were supported by university leadership, the campus community, and the surrounding Indigenous communities. During this journey, we committed to a creative process in collaboration with community; our journey was grounded by mutual respect, common goals, and a commitment to building and maintaining good relatives.

Jackie Sieppert

My name is Jackie Sieppert. I am also known as Oot'soo Piik'sii [Shore Bird], a name that Elders Reg and Rose Crowshoe gifted to me in 2018. I am a social worker, an educator, a father, and a grandfather. I am also the product of homesteader families, settlers who came to Canada with hope and gratitude for the opportunity to build new lives. They were as hard as the soil that they tilled, absolutely driven to create a bright future for their children, and the hardest-working people whom I have ever known. As a child in the Hand Hills of southern Alberta, I revered my grandparents. I believed that they taught me everything I would ever need to know in life. In most ways, they did.

As an adult, though, I now know that there were things my home-steader families did not teach me. I have learned that, like all of you, I am a treaty person. I have learned that I knew nothing of Indigenous communities or the historical relationships that we have had with those communities. I have learned as a social worker that we continue to see Indigenous peoples marginalized and over-represented in our corrections and child welfare systems.

Most of all, I have learned about the impact of loss and the legacy of residential schools. As a father, I have experienced the relentless, un-forgiving loss of a child. Yet I am here to say that I have no capacity to imagine the loss endured by Indigenous families who saw their children removed from them without notice or reason. Families who were not al-lowed to see their children. Families who witnessed the conscious process of assimilation that stole their children's love, culture, identity, and future. Families who learned that their children were abused in so many ways. This is why—as a social worker and father—I am so passionate about *ii' taa'poh'to'p*. I am an ally who cares deeply about creating hope and new futures for those children and their families.

Being an ally has been essential to my career at the University of Calgary, now over three decades long. During this period, I have been priv-ileged to be a faculty member in the Faculty of Social Work, and between 2010 and 2020 I served as its dean. It was while I was in this leadership role that the provost asked me to join the Indigenous Strategy's Steering Committee and to co-chair the Working Group tasked with developing the strategy itself. Looking back, it was a transformative experience. I re-main engaged on this journey and hope to earn the honour of being called a neighbour of Indigenous communities.

Backside view of *ii' taa'poh'to'p* tipi. June 29, 2018. University of Calgary. Photo credit: Riley Brandt, UCalgary.

Appendix: Videos

CHAPTER 3

3.1 In a Good Way

This short video provides an overview of the Indigenous proverb— "in a good way"—as explained by Jacqueline Ottmann. This teaching is a foundational key concept of the University of Calgary Indigenous Strategy.

University of Calgary. 2017. "In a Good Way." Edited by Trevor Alberts. Calgary, AB, November. Video, 1 min., 2 sec.

https://digitalcollections.ucalgary.ca/AssetLink/ w3ft3p433ii73wa366736v8364nsy88q/In-a-Good-Way.mp4.mp4.

CHAPTER 4

4.1 The Journey

This short video provides an overview of the University of Calgary's journey towards the development of the Indigenous Strategy *ii' taa'poh'to'p*.

University of Calgary. 2017. "The Journey." Edited by Trevor Alberts. Calgary, AB, November. Video, 3 min, 48 sec.

https://digitalcollections.ucalgary.ca/AssetLink/ tao4n7rg22f17xk3330a655i7402vf4l/The-Journey-2017-.mp4.mp4.

CHAPTER 6

6.1 Transformation

This short video, featuring Piikani Elder Reg Crowshoe, provides an overview of the cultural symbol and traditional teaching for the concept of transformation.

University of Calgary. 2017. "Transformation." Edited by Trevor Alberts. Calgary, AB, November. Video, 31 sec.

https://digitalcollections.ucalgary.ca/ AssetLink/3lno4f4kj42i3ytbjr6gdv4115xxe276/Transformation.mp4.mp4.

6.2 Renewal

This short video, featuring Piikani Elder Reg Crowshoe, provides an overview of the cultural symbol and traditional teaching for the concept of renewal.

University of Calgary. 2017. "Renewal." Edited by Trevor Alberts. Calgary, AB, November. Video, 32 sec.

https://digitalcollections.ucalgary.ca/ AssetLink/2t44yp6ts5Orlb545ska1rcf2mOvupuv/Renewal.mp4.mp4.

6.3 Shared Space

This short video, featuring Piikani Elder Reg Crowshoe, provides an overview of the cultural symbol and traditional teaching for the concept of shared space.

University of Calgary. 2017. "Shared Space." Edited by Trevor Alberts. Calgary, AB, November. Video, 44 sec.

https://digitalcollections.ucalgary.ca/AssetLink/ Oo20qOt1Oww1p1181y6nrre2438jOm7c/Shared-Space.mp4.mp4.

6.4 Ways of Knowing

This short video, featuring Piikani Elder Reg Crowshoe, provides an overview of the cultural symbol and traditional teaching for one of the four visionary circles titled "Ways of Knowing."

University of Calgary. 2017. "Ways of Knowing." Edited by Trevor Alberts. Calgary, AB, November. Video, 45 sec.

https://digitalcollections.ucalgary.ca/AssetLink/ x5n0674c5348604fhbi480g3u75l4wjq/Ways-of-Knowing.mp4.mp4.

6.5 Ways of Doing

This short video, featuring Piikani Elder Reg Crowshoe, provides an overview of the cultural symbol and traditional teaching for one of the four visionary circles titled "Ways of Doing."

University of Calgary. 2017. "Ways of Doing." Edited by Trevor Alberts. Calgary, AB, November. Video, 34 sec.

https://digitalcollections.ucalgary.ca/AssetLink/ 1u035j5e0e5yg86qry288687xah8xpck/Ways-of-Doing.mp4.mp4.

6.6 Ways of Connecting

This short video, featuring Piikani Elder Reg Crowshoe, provides an overview of the cultural symbol and traditional teaching for one of the four visionary circles titled "Ways of Connecting."

University of Calgary. 2017. "Ways of Connecting." Edited by Trevor Alberts. Calgary, AB, November. Video, 37 sec.

https://digitalcollections.ucalgary.ca/AssetLink/ tc2451s4by7p8jop6j68dgtr1r1if0l1/Ways-of-Connecting.mp4.mp4.

6.7 Ways of Being

This short video, featuring Piikani Elder Reg Crowshoe, provides an overview of the cultural symbol and traditional teaching for one of the four visionary circles titled "Ways of Being."

University of Calgary. 2017. "Ways of Being." Edited by Trevor Alberts. Calgary, AB, November. Video, 29 sec.

https://digitalcollections.ucalgary.ca/AssetLink/ hqknt753ff5hj04j58db6g6c5d7xun12/Ways-of-Being.mp4.mp4.

CHAPTER 7

7.1 Andy Black Water, The Name

This short video provides the cultural teaching about the gifting of the Blackfoot name *ii' taa'poh'to'p* to the University of Calgary for the Indigenous Strategy. The name was gifted, with an affiliated cultural teaching, by the late Kainai Elder Andy Black Water.

University of Calgary. 2017. "Andy Black Water, The Name." Edited by Trevor Alberts. Calgary, AB, November. Video, 1 min, 7 sec.

https://digitalcollections.ucalgary.ca/AssetLink/
wlbf6r3dv63042nq65353m3yt7wup8td/Andy-BlackWater-The-Name.
mp4.mp4.

CHAPTER 8

8.1 Tipi Painting, Timelapse Video

This short video shows the creation of the *ii' taa'poh'to'p* tipi, from the drawing through to the final painting of the Indigenous strategy cultural symbols on to large scale tipi canvas. The *ii' taa'poh'to'p* tipi was designed and transferred to the University of Calgary by Piikani Elder Reg Crowshoe.

University of Calgary. 2018. "Teepee Painting, Timelapse Video." Calgary, AB, August. Video, 57 sec.

https://digitalcollections.ucalgary.ca/AssetLink/
yxg6i5oo1q7ybq3tdauqfs372h688gyi/Timelapse_-UCalgary-tipi-
painting-and-raising.mp4.mp4.

8.2 Tipi Painting, Campfire Chats Partnership Event at Stampede 2018

This short video shows painting of the *ii' taa'poh'to'p* tipi at a Campfire Chats community event hosted by the University of Calgary in partnership with the Calgary Stampede in honor of National Indigenous Peoples Day on June 21, 2018. The video highlights the final painting of Indigenous strategy cultural symbols on to large scale tipi canvas.

University of Calgary. 2018. "Tipi Painting, Campfire Chats Partnership Event at Stampede 2018." Calgary, Alberta, June. Video, 1 min., 38 sec.

https://digitalcollections.ucalgary.ca/AssetLink/
ww3a42xjo6w2n1ijkjoq73qnx05r0v6j/Campfire-Chats---Tipi-at-
Stampede.mp4.mp4.

Video Acknowledgements

VIDEOGRAPHERS

3.1–7.1

Trevor Alberts, Senior Producer, Director, and President, Arcade Video

8.1–8.2

V Strategies

VIDEO PROJECT LEADS

3.1, 4.1, and 7.1

Gillian Edwards, Manager, Institutional Communications, Strategic Communications, University Relations, University of Calgary

6.1–6.7

Susan Mide Kiss, Senior Director, Community Engagement, University Relations, University of Calgary

8.1–8.2

University Relations, University of Calgary

www.ingramcontent.com/pod-product-compliance
Lightning Source LLC
Chambersburg PA
CBHW040148270326
41929CB00025B/3425